POLITICAL PARTIES
IN THE UNITED STATES

St. Martin's Series

in American Politics

———

EARL LATHAM

General Editor

POLITICAL
PARTIES
IN THE
UNITED STATES

Allan P. Sindler

CORNELL UNIVERSITY

ST. MARTIN'S PRESS · NEW YORK

To the late V. O. Key, Jr.—
whose penetrating analyses of American politics
have taught and stimulated so many of us

Preface

This volume is too brief to permit full coverage of the field of American political parties. Instead, a few topics have been selected with an eye to illuminating some of the major characteristics of the American party system. After establishing the interrelationship of party and governmental systems, roughly defining party, and setting forth its major functions, the rest of the first chapter explains and applies one way of classifying American party systems. I chose "degree of competition" because of its substantive value and because it illustrates problems facing quantitative analysis in the social sciences. Testing the usefulness of the classification scheme, Chapters II and III dissect two-partyism as against one- and multi-partyism—in its operations and in the conditions that cause its presence or absence. The fourth chapter discusses some key characteristics of America's two major parties, and then explores the role of party within the Congress and the electorate. The final chapter appraises the major conflicting evaluations of the American party system, and speculates on trends that might promote certain party reforms.

Since the primary audience for this study is the nonspecialist student of American government and politics, I have discussed these topics in self-sufficient terms that do not require extensive knowledge of parties from the reader. My approach is empirical analysis, and sequences of reasoned arguments link related points to a common larger theme. When warranted, normative discussions have also been introduced, especially in dealing with party in the broad context of its governmental setting. I believe, contrary to some current strong trends in the discipline, that so long as normative and empirical concerns are kept distinct and unconfused, a political scientist need not make an exclusive choice between the two approaches.

In the pages that follow are frequent references to the politics of the South. These reflect my belief that political patterns and trends in the South provide the materials for a deeper understanding of the party system. My own continuing interest in that area stems largely from the opportunities for broad party analysis inherent in a close study of Southern politics. Accordingly, Southern events are here probed less for their intrinsic interest than for their capacity to illuminate the nature and operation of one-partyism, the relationships of national to state politics, and the decentralized organization of the national parties.

I began the detailed planning of this study during the latter part of my 1963-64 fellowship at the Center for Advanced Study in the Behavioral Sciences in Stanford, California. My gratitude for having had that unharried year of professional reinvigoration is matched only by my regret that it is over. But this book really is the product of my experiences over the years in teaching American parties to university undergraduate and graduate students. I am particularly grateful to the students who made genuine use of the educational process by advancing views, arguments, and evidence contrary to mine, compelling me more than occasionally to refine or alter my own analysis and judgments. Many parts of this study are the better for those past exchanges, and disputatious readers are warmly invited to follow that rewarding practice.

ALLAN P. SINDLER

Ithaca, New York
February 1966

Contents

POLITICAL PARTIES
IN THE UNITED STATES

Chapter I

PARTY
AND AMERICAN
PARTY SYSTEMS

Although George Washington's warnings of the "baneful effects of the spirit of faction" expressed a fear common to many of the Founding Fathers, the fact is that contemporary American government leaders are partisan leaders. And virtually all other national leaders in today's world are partisan leaders also. The political party is thus located closer to the center and not at the periphery of modern governments. Party systems and operations differ significantly from one country to another, but in each the centrality of party to the character of the overall political system remains high. Hence an analysis of the party system of a single nation—the United States in this study—

cannot serve to illuminate all party systems elsewhere. But it can and should be structured to provide an examination of the larger contextual political system of which the party is an integral part.

The Linkage of Party and Democracy

In the evolution of Western constitutionalism, the development of party has been broadly associated with that of democracy. Competing cabals in the days of absolute monarchs eventually evolved into representative assemblies, initially limited in suffrage base and scope of party organization. Both those dimensions were subsequently enlarged so that party organization reached outside the government structures themselves. Accompanying these developments was the acceptance of the concept of a "loyal opposition," a self-denying and tolerant doctrine which still falls notoriously short of universal adherence. Once the concept of legitimate opposition to the party in power was implemented by institutional arrangements, party competition became a central ingredient of democracy. As Clinton Rossiter has asserted, "parties and democracy arose together; they have lived and prospered in a closely symbiotic relationship; and if one of them should ever weaken and die, the other would die with it."[1] Note that, as the adjective "symbiotic" implies, the relationships between party and democracy are mutual and reciprocal, not solely in one direction. Whether either has shaped the other more, or whether either can be altered without change in the other, are important questions to which at least partial answers will be offered later.

Many hostile critics of party, including those among the Founding Fathers, implicitly recognized the close linkage of party and democracy. When they indicted party as a nationally divisive force, as perverting the public interest by its pursuit of selfish partisan goals, or as undermining the legislators' moral independence of action, they were only partly aiming at alleged evils of party. They were also opposing an undiluted majoritarianism of a mass-based democracy. They rightly perceived that the populist type of government they disliked would be promoted by institutionalizing "the spirit of faction." Such a view is by no means buried in the distant past. Some of the current voices raised against party are animated by an abiding distrust of political conflict as such, or of popular politics as inherently injurious to the public good

---

[1] Clinton Rossiter, *Parties and Politics in America* (Ithaca: Cornell University Press, 1960), p. 67.

and to American values (as they understand those terms). These moderns, unable to attack democracy directly because of the sanctity which nearly all the world's peoples impute to that form of goverment, vent their dissatisfactions on the political party, accurately perceiving party as the handmaiden of democracy.

In his classic Tenth Paper of *The Federalist* James Madison set forth a position right to the point under discussion. Madison equated good government with the maintenance of liberty, and then acknowledged that parties, as the vehicles for diverse human needs, interests, and outlooks, would develop inevitably in a context of liberty. Conversely, any attempt to suppress party would repress the expression of naturally diverse interests, and consequently would fatally impair liberty. The "symbiotic relationship" between party and democracy—to use Rossiter's term again—prohibited Madison from choosing one without the other, and confined him to opt for both or for neither. Madison's love of liberty thus compelled him to accept the existence of party, while his fear of party then led him to discuss institutional and other ways to contain its harmful effects.

The majority of Americans today share perhaps, in a looser and intuitive fashion, Madison's insight on the intimate relationship between party and democracy. Yet the predominant complexion of American attitudes toward the political party is a grudging acceptance of party, a dwelling on its defects, a search for ways to circumscribe party power and influence—a direction also enunciated by Madison. These attitudes reflect a deep-seated mistrust of politics and government, but they may also reflect, paradoxically, a tacitly hopeful view of the capacity of the political system to better the human condition. Consider, for example, the reaction upon learning that a public office holder has abused his office for private gain. Is not our outrage based in part on our expecting public officials to operate by ethical standards superior to those governing, say, business or personal conduct? The severity of our adverse reactions may be triggered by our subconscious faith that the sphere of political activity calls for the best in man. Popular negativism toward party may grow from a similar feeling of a faith betrayed, in that many sense that party has not come near enough to fulfilling its unique contribution to the workings of democracy.

For present purposes we need not pursue this line of speculation, but merely acknowledge that these negative appraisals of party shape party operations in important ways subsequently to be described. The perspective on party adopted in this study subscribes to the Madisonian position on the functional indispensability of party to democracy, and considers that issue foreclosed. Our broad question thus becomes: what kind of party system best implements the American political system? Implicit in that question is the view that the Madisonian and popular conceptions underrate the positive role of party. This study will be concerned, then, with describing and assessing the strengths and weaknesses of the American party system, accepting democracy's need for some viable party system as an unalterable given.

A Rough Definition of Party

Defining of terms in the social sciences is risky, most obviously because the definitions are neither watertight nor complete. A further danger is that the content of the definition will be taken as a statement of the desired social objective, so that when reality is perceived to deviate from the definition the former wrongly may be assumed deficient and to require remedying. These risks take on added meaning in the case of the political party, even when, as here, we focus on a single nation's experience. The term "party" as used professionally and popularly has covered a wide range of phenomena and behaviors: amorphous electoral groupings in the mass population, the organizational structure of the party, the public office holders or the legislative or executive segment thereof, the minor as well as the major parties, or all of the foregoing without distinction as to component parts, etc. In light of these general and special risks, the reader should understand the utility of presenting here only a "rough definition" of party, one which makes no pretense of overcoming the limitations on definition just noted. If the rough definition of party clarifies and guides far more than it obscures or misleads, its present purpose will be well served.

The need to distinguish party from its competitors, such as factions and interest groups (popularly called "pressure groups"), directs our attention to certain key elements of party. The essential "reason for being" of party is political: parties exist for politics on a full-time, overt, and continuous basis. Many interest groups are also in politics, but more sporadically, and often their political functions comprise the lesser portion of their total complex of purposes and activities. Moreover, in many interest groups a leadership decision to commit the group's name and resources to political action may provoke internal dispute. Some trade union members or some doctors in the American Medical Association invariably question the propriety of their group undertaking political or partisan activity, an attitude unthinkable for members of a political party.

It is this pervasively political character of party that impels it to devote its energies to secure political power: the objective of party is the control of government, a more extensive goal than the interest group's. If this characteristic of party tends to have near universal reference, then we can link particular party systems to particular political contexts by stressing the legitimate means by which control of government may be achieved. In the American setting the required means is by control of public office, thus involving the party centrally in contesting popular elections and mobilizing diverse electoral support on behalf of whatever goals will attract the requisite organizational manpower and votes.

Factions are also explicitly political, but they can be distinguished from party by emphasizing the party as a "stable organization." Factions customarily have a less elaborated and patterned internal structure than party; that is, the formal organization of party is more fully developed and durable. Party organization is expected to be more stable and continuing over a run of successive elections, providing a more constant and meaningful reference point for voters than faction. The important differences in the capacity of party and faction to structure politics for the guidance of voters will occupy our attention in the next chapter.

Our concept of party rejects treating party in terms of issue attachments, one classic version of which is Burke's description of party as "a body of men united, for promoting by their joint endeavors the national interest, upon some particular principle on which they are all agreed." (In fairness to Burke, recall that a party in his day was really a legislative caucus in opposition to a governing cabinet.) Burke's view is excessively preoccupied with policy, and implies a false distinction between agencies pursuing power goals and those seeking policy goals. Parties in fact attempt to secure both goals, although the mixture varies. We apply the term "machine," for example, to a party that virtually abandons policy goals in favor of the achievement of power; we point to a minor party or to an interest group as examples of political groups enamored of policy goals to the seeming exclusion of seeking power. The Burkean definition fits the latter examples better than it does the American major parties.

The elements that define party here advanced do not overlook the policy orientation of party, but rather treat it as one of several means to the power end of party: the control of government through the pursuit of election victories. The same observation applies to a concept of party as an electoral alliance of various socioeconomic groups. The material drives of party tend to be more enduring than any commitment in the abstract to ideology or to any particular policy position, and hence they merit heavy though not exclusive emphasis in any definition of party.[2] A stress on party as a bureaucratic organization, with internal structural relationships and hierarchies of leaders and followers, also underscores the shaping of the party's form by its concern to contest for power.

By affirming the importance of the power-seeking aspect of party we do not undercut our ability to distinguish constitutional from totalitarian parties. Party, after all, does not operate in a vacuum, and the political context within which party functions leaves its durable and often idiosyncratic impress on particular party systems. The means by which party tries to capture power varies all the way from persuasion to force, from genuine to spurious elections, from competition to monopoly. The presence uniformly of hierarchical organization within parties does not preclude the analyst from inquiring further into such important dimensions as the degree of centralization, the provisions for registering dissent, the openness of leadership and candidate recruitment, the scope and nature of party membership, and the like.

Nor does an emphasis on the power goals of party foreclose the question of the positive contribution of party to the overall political system. The design of American government, after all, is largely premised on the belief that the public good can be effectively served by individual pursuit of private and selfish goals, *if* this self-seeking is properly channeled through institutional and other devices. The Framers were the very opposite of utopians on this point. They did not urge that environmental changes would eradicate human ambition and conflict; they accepted ambition and conflict as given, and then sought institutional ways to harness private selfishness into service for the public good. So, too, classical liberal economics posited a socially

---

[2] For a logical analysis of party and voter in terms of a "rational behavior" calculus akin to that used in economics for the study of "economic man," see Anthony Downs, *An Economic Theory of Democracy* (New York: Harper & Brothers, 1957). The perspective on party here is neither as exclusively power-oriented nor as rigorously applied as that of Downs.

beneficial distribution of goods and services in the wake of the economic self-seeking of individuals choosing in response to the impersonal forces of the market. The usefulness to the political system of the by-products of the American party's pursuit of power thus remains an open question warranting continuing attention in this study.

Key Functions of Party

To clarify this beginning discussion of party functions, it would be helpful initially to sort out several aspects. First, in line with the point previously made, party performs certain self-promoting functions which, incidentally but inevitably, affect the overall system within which party operates.[3] Suppose a local political party supported, for purposes of election gain, the candidacy of a qualified Negro for important local office. This action would have implications for the larger system which the party may or may not have intended or anticipated. It would affect, at the minimum, the openness and receptivity of the political process to minority groups, the political consciousness and participation of the Negro citizenry, perhaps the issue positions of the party, and the like. This one action, then, would have self-promoting and system-affecting consequences, and it remains analytically useful to keep that distinction clearly in mind.

Second, pending later argument let us assume that the chances of party effectively discharging both those types of functions are enhanced under two-party competition and depressed by an imbalance of party strength. That is, party will more often pursue its self-promoting ends in ways beneficial to the public good when each party is forced to operate under a real competitive threat from the other. In this sense party competition plays as basic a role in political science analysis as the competition among firms does in economics.

As a third and final separable aspect of this topic, the party functions we shall treat are those necessary to the satisfactory operation of a democracy. Hence the better they are performed the more effective the democracy, and because they are necessary functions, some agencies will attempt to perform them. We believe, for reasons again to be

---

[3] This distinction between the self-promoting and system-affecting functions of party is a familiar one in political science analysis, allowing for the differing terminology of analysts. To give one example, Frank J. Sorauf borrows and applies the terms "manifest" and "latent" party functions in a good discussion of this same distinction. See his *Political Parties in the American System* (Boston: Little, Brown and Company, 1964), esp. pp. 2-6, 8-12, 164-167.

set forth later, that a competitive two-party system can better handle most of those functions than can alternative agencies, such as interest groups, factions, or community elites. Empirically, however, it is indisputably clear that American parties have not established anything like a monopoly in controlling these functions. The discussion of party functions which follows should not therefore be misunderstood as a description of what in fact American parties do. Rather it suggests what the fullest potential for the party's role is, from a view that imbeds the party in the context of constitutional two-partyism, but abstracts it from any particular nation. The extent to which parties in the American setting actually realize that potential is thus a question left open for subsequent determination.

Since the party's target is the control of government through success in elections, its self-promoting functions necessarily involve presenting candidates for public office, and amassing sufficient popular support behind those candidates to make the party a serious and durable contender for power. To secure the requisite electoral support party must attract a persistent following, and others less partisanly loyal, by shaping their perceptions of political norms, issues, events, parties, candidates, and policies, and by encouraging psychological and material ties to the party as symbol and as organization. The party's efforts to proselytize, reinforce, and manipulate are in the service of the ultimate aim of the capture and exercise of government power, which are the maximum functions performable by party.

The effects of these self-promoting functions on the overall system are so pervasive that we cannot attempt a complete listing and rely instead on selective example and emphasis. Consider, for instance, the broader implications of the party's selfish function of presenting candidates for office. By its actions in this sphere party inevitably shapes the recruitment patterns by which the political system obtains its leadership, the qualities of political leadership considered most relevant by the citizenry, and quite literally the kind and calibre of personnel who occupy elective office at virtually all political levels.

In like manner the need for mass support involves party unceasingly and intimately in the larger functions of molding and representing opinions and interests. Our inability as a mass citizenry to initiate or frame policy means that we can perform effectively largely by reacting to policy choices prestructured for us. Party is one of the most influential of these prestructuring forces, providing us with guidelines and answers to the following sorts of basic queries. Of the infinity of events occurring, which penetrate our consciousness as having to do with politics? Of those, which command our attention as most salient? What interpretation of these salient political events, of candidate abilities, of issues in dispute, is given us by party? In sum, our awareness and knowledge of politics and our perception of political phenomena are powerfully conditioned by party. Party represents as well as molds interests when it orders political reality and proffers political alternatives. Because each party tries to construct and maintain a majority coalition of interests, and because they compete, parties act as primary agents of both cleavage and consensus in the society. And as an ongoing organization attracting the loyalty and attention of its followers, party satisfies a range of emotional and cognitive needs for many.

The supreme potential of party and its broadest impact on the larger system lies in what party does with the government power it captures by winning elections. Theoretically party can be the principal means of constitutionalizing politics; through party, proposed and enacted government policy can derive from the consent of the governed as filtered through periodic competitive elections. Party, in other words, can be the major intermediary mechanism between the people and formal government institutions, facilitating the translation of popular interests and needs into authoritative legislative and administrative enactments. If party adheres to that role regularly and thoroughly, it may perform an additional major democratizing function, because it tends to inflate the importance of sheer numbers (voters) to offset other types of political influence possessed by persons or groups of wealth, education, expertise, and so on. In the American setting of a separation of powers, the American party is capable, on paper at least, of ameliorating the strained relationship inherent in independent executive and legislative branches.

Moving from this rather abstract discussion of key party functions to the real world, we readily see that the degree to which party actually executes these functions varies greatly. For instance, the strategic role of party in transmuting popular interests into government policy has been termed by many writers the "brokerage" function. The concept of party as broker may suggest, however, different expected behaviors ranging from a passive and neutral representational role to a more aggressive one as a major autonomous center initiating the formulation of public issues. Some of the disagreement between critics and defenders of the American party system, as will be shown in the final chapter, turns on which concept of brokerage is favored.

Although the party's major functions are separable for analytic purposes, as a practical matter they are often intertwined. It can be argued, for example, that party can control government effectively only insofar as it is clear about its policy goals, which in turn requires party in performing its electing function to structure voter opinion meaningfully. The reverse relationship also can be urged: unless party can control government action and be identified with government policies, it cannot hope to organize or express public opinion effectively. What perspective is taken on this assertion of a "fusion" of electing-representing-governing functions is again one of the sticking points in the quarrel between defenders and critics of the present American party system.

Finally, note that in practice the party's satisfaction of one function may drastically inhibit its ability to satisfy another function. At the logical extreme, for instance, faithful representation of all shades of opinion in a diverse society might well incapacitate the parties in their governing function. Again, if a party considered its task of mobilizing electoral majorities solely in arithmetical terms, its pursuit of votes might well exaggerate either its cleavage-provoking or consensus-promoting functions. Perhaps the most chronic of the possible conflicts of functions is that which pits the electing function against the presentation of clear policy alternatives to the electorate. Both these functions cannot be equally served by a party that discovers that the issues it supports, or might like to support, are unpopular and handicap its election fortunes. We shall consider this problem in the closing chapter, when we discuss the prescriptions offered by the doctrine of party government.

Classifying Party Systems by Degree of Competition

To speak of a "party system," as we have, is to refer to a set of component elements, each functioning interdependently with the others within an inclusive whole. Were any of the important elements greatly changed, the whole would be expected to undergo major change in its nature and operation. Accordingly, party systems may be classified by reference to some of those component elements. If this study dealt comparatively with the party systems of many nations the attempt to classify those systems would include many or all of the following components: the loyalty of parties to the ongoing form of government, the scope of party membership, the spread and intensity of party ideology, the number of competitive parties, the relation of party leaders to government leaders, the internal structure of the parties, the extent of suffrage, the predominant political attitudes of the citizenry, and the like.[4] Since we concentrate here only on the American political context, it is neither necessary nor appropriate to include all such elements. In fact, a simple but useful classification scheme can be based on just one element, on the understanding that what is excluded may be reintroduced in our later discussion of the characteristics shared by the major parties.

Party systems in America may appropriately be classified according to the number of parties that seriously compete in elections. The well-known categories resulting are one-party, two-party, and multiparty (three or more) systems, with the classifier retaining the option of making more refined breakdowns within each category. Obviously this classification base is limited to just one of the several functions of party, but given the emphasis American parties place on pursuit of election victory, this deficiency is not too grave. The adequacy of any classification scheme, however, hinges on demonstration and not on argumentation. To be useful, a party classification base must distinguish between and direct attention to significantly different party systems. Hence, given the classification scheme just adopted, we shall frequently refer to the important behavior differences evident in one-, two-, and multi-party systems. We first, however, examine how the classification scheme is worked out, because we can understand the substantive findings only in the context of the methodology employed. And a close dissection of the party classification scheme sensitizes the reader to some of the difficulties and pitfalls in empirical and quantitative analysis in the social sciences.

The determination of how many parties "seriously compete" for elective government offices is an empirical inquiry, centered on investigating past election returns for various offices. The analyst must choose the measure of competition, the offices to study, and the time period. He must establish quantitative boundary lines, designating each of the resulting categories to denote a different party system indexed by a different degree or kind of interparty competition. While this proce-

---

[4] For recent attempts to develop such bases of classification, see Maurice Duverger, *Political Parties* (New York: John Wiley & Sons, 1954) and Avery Leiserson, *Parties and Politics* (New York: Alfred A. Knopf, 1958).

dure may sound simple, many difficulties and disagreements among analysts exist. Perhaps the most helpful advance warning is to stress that an investigator's conclusions on degree of party competition are products entirely of his measures and categories, and should be read only with reference to them.

There is no point to a lengthy cataloguing of all the problems in classifying parties by the measure of election competition, and the following examples should suffice. Some arbitrariness and subjectivity must at times enter into fixing the quantitative cut-off points, if only because we do not know enough about the actual workings of diverse party systems. Suppose, for example, that one classification design adopts as the outermost boundary for a "competitive" party system one in which the majority party has won no more than 60 percent of the elections involved, and another classifier chooses to use an outermost limit of 65 percent. The state of our present knowledge justifies the need to distinguish between the category of competitive states and that of, let us say, "modified one-party" states. But we cannot say whether the 60 or the 65 percent figure is the proper line of demarcation, and the fact that most researchers might prefer one or the other testifies simply to a standardization and not to a validation of that measure.

Representation also introduces complications. Should a measurement of party competition in congressional politics deal with the total popular vote, the popular vote on an election-district basis, total seats in the chamber, or what? Further complexities derive from the institutional arrangements associated with separation of powers and federalism. Should interparty competition be determined by reference to elections for president, Senate, House, governor, state treasurer, state legislature, mayor, or whom? If the findings were roughly equivalent no matter what the offices examined, the question would become moot. But the findings do vary by office, and there is no way to prove which provides the "truest" measure of interparty competition. About all that can be said is that some research purposes are better served by using one set of offices rather than another, or by selecting party percentage of popular vote rather than of seats won, and so on. Once again, then, it is important to keep the findings closely linked to the particular methodology used.

A heavily used measure of competition, which consists of determining which parties won what proportion of a designated total of elections for a specified office, raises another type of problem. The closer the parties approach to equal proportions of victory, the more competitive the party system is said to be. For refined analysis, this obviously gross measure could be improved on. A majority party facing an opposition party that consistently secured 40 percent of the vote would behave differently than if the opposition could gain only 15 percent of the vote. To facilitate distinguishing between those two types of party systems, the measure of competition must supplement a reliance on the proportions of election victory or defeat by assessing the strength of the minority party. Two-party situations may also require more refined classification and measurement; for example, distinguishing between lengthy periods of control first by one party and then by the other from a more regularly alternating pattern of party control. For example, if each of two parties won ten of twenty elections, the finding by use of the initial gross measure would be a 50 percent figure, signifying maximum competition. But that same figure could also mean that the first ten elections were won by one party and the next ten by the other, or that at each election the in-party lost and the out-party won. Hence the gross measure should be supplemented by some technique to gauge the frequency of party change. The constant requirement, then, is to develop measures and categories, using only the quantitative data of election results, that can account for at least the party systems generally acknowledged to exist, and perhaps identify others more obscure as well.

Findings

In presidential politics the predominant pattern, if we focus on the nation as the unit of analysis and if we use popular vote distributions, is clearly competitive two-partyism. From 1828 to the present with few exceptions the two parties together have persistently polled upward of 90 percent of the national popular vote—that is, there has been little multi-partyism; and they have persistently divided that vote between themselves within a 60-40 percent range—that is, there has been little one-partyism. Judgments of the vigor of this competition depend heavily on the measuring device employed. If we link the sequence of Federalist, Whig, and Republican parties on the one side, and the Jeffersonian, Democratic-Republican, and Democratic parties on the other, each side has won about the same number of presidential elections; vigorous competition has obtained. If, however, the supplementary measure of the frequency of change in party control of the White House is applied, the result is different. Successive eras of one-party victory seem to make up the overall pattern of two-party competition. Allowing for the fact that political historians would not unitedly endorse any one particular breakdown, the following might produce as much agreement as any: a period of Federalist control up to 1800, followed by a Jeffersonian and Democratic period through the outbreak of the Civil War, succeeded by a lengthy period of Republican rule until the Great Depression, followed by a period of Democratic dominance still with us currently.

A broadly similar pattern of two-partyism characterizes congressional politics. Since third-party strength has been greater in presidential than in congressional races, there has been little multi-partyism in the latter. The two major parties have nearly always split the national congressional popular vote within a 60-40 percent limit, thereby minimizing the occurrence of one-partyism. Even though a defeated party tends to get a lower proportion of chamber seats than of popular vote, it has usually been able to hold on to an impressive minority of seats. In the Democratic heyday from 1932-1944 the Republicans retained an average of just under one-third of the Senate seats and just over one-third of the House seats. In House elections held at the same time as presidential elections, the party direction of vote change—using national popular vote as the election data—tends to be the same in both, with the qualification that the party shift in presidential vote from election to election has tended to be wider. Hence the 1956 outcomes, in which Eisenhower was returned to the presidency by a larger margin than in 1952 but the Democrats were able to retain their control of the Congress, constituted a rare exception. At House elections held at presidential midterm, the party in control of the presidency tends to lose seats, and at times the loss has been sufficient to shift party control of the House. Therefore the party competition pattern for the House, with respect to party control of the chamber, has exhibited a greater degree of party alternation than that uncovered for party control of the presidency.

Findings on party competition at sub-national levels are not only relevant in their own right, but are necessary to clarify understanding the interparty balance in national politics. National two-partyism, after all, could rest on a combination of mostly one-party or mostly two-party units. In view of the plethora of offices and units that might be investigated, we shall have to confine our attention to a handful: House districts in House elections, and states in presidential and gubernatorial elections.

Relevant party data on House elections may be inferred indirectly from Professor Ewing's study on a related subject, one which computed the winning candidate's margin of victory for all House elections, by districts, for the 26 elections from 1896-1946 inclusive.[5] Ewing's categories of elections in which the winner had a thirty-percentage-point-or-higher plurality margin (from 65-35 to 100-0 percent vote division in a two-party race) represent weakly contested or uncontested elections. We here additionally infer that it was the same party that consistently won by these lopsided margins, and not different parties winning in alternating elections—that is, that these elections were held in durable one-party districts. By comparable inference, we assume that the category of competitive elections, characterized by plurality margins of less than twenty percentage points for the winner (within 60-40 percent vote division in a two-party race), and the category of closely competitive elections, characterized by plurality margins of less than ten percentage points (within 55-45 percent vote division in a two-party race), also represented competitive two-party districts. These assumptions are doubtless subject to a margin of error, greater in the case of competitive than of weakly contested elections, but the findings nonetheless are a rough index of the magnitude of the various patterns of interparty strength.

Of the more than ten thousand elections tabulated, 27 percent were closely competitive, 47 percent were competitive (which includes the preceding category), and at the other end 40 percent were weakly contested or uncontested. Sectional variations existed, of course, the most notable being the high proportion (82 percent) of weakly contested or uncontested elections in the South and the high proportion (77 percent) of competitive elections in the five Border states. If Southern elections are excluded, then the rest of the nation had closely competitive elections in 34 percent, and weakly contested or uncontested elections in 25 percent, of all elections. While most Southern elections thus were one-party in character, one-partyism was by no means confined entirely to the South. On a national basis, the number of "unsafe" House districts characterized by closely competitive parties

---

[5] Cortez A. M. Ewing, "Primaries as Real Elections," *Southwestern Social Science Quarterly*, 29 (March 1949), 293-298. Ewing's disregard of party in his classification scheme reflected his concern with the question of what proportion of general elections were so ineffectively contested as to make the nominating stage (the primary election) the decisive or "real" election.

and uncertain election outcomes has ranged, for the period of recent and current politics, from about 100 to 125.[6]

State party patterns in presidential and gubernatorial politics are revealed jointly in a study by Professor Schlesinger, which applied the same measure to both arenas for, respectively, 1872-1948 and 1870-1950.[7] Competitive two-party states were defined as those in which neither party had won more than 65 percent of the elections; that classification was then further refined by reference to how often the state voted for a different party than in the previous election. "Continuously competitive" signified a frequency of party alternation of over 40 percent. Whereas the theoretical maximum was 100 percent—party overturn at every election—the actual maximum uncovered was 60 percent. "Cyclically competitive" signified a rate of party alternation of less than 40 percent. Three categories of one-party states rounded out Schlesinger's classification scheme, all of them characterized by the fact that one party had won more than 65 percent of all the elections. They were distinguished from each other by different brackets of party alternation rates, which indexed different relationships between majority and minority party. "Cyclical one-party" characterized situations in which the minority party was able to win consecutively for short periods of control. "Predominant one-party" meant that the minority party was able to win only isolated victories without succeeding itself in office. The final category was "completely one-party," in which the majority party won virtually all elections, and the party alternation rate was therefore zero or close to it.

Schlesinger's basic findings are set forth in Table 1, with the initials R and D referring respectively to the Republican and Democratic parties. By Schlesinger's measure, only 13 of the 48 states fell into either category of competitive states, and 35 states were assigned to

---

[6] For a full understanding of these findings, note that the competitiveness of election outcomes in House districts can be affected by the district boundaries, and that the majority party in the state legislature often sets the geography of representation to enhance its partisan advantage and to reduce the number of closely competitive districts. (This point lacks relevance when the focus is on the state, since state boundaries remain fixed.) Even if House elections are appraised in terms of party proportions of national popular vote, this point remains pertinent because the question of how many voted for which party is affected by the competitive complexion of the party situation within each district. There is not, after all, any national popular vote in House elections, except as an artificial construct of the analyst; there is only the aggregate of 435 separate House elections.

[7] Joseph A. Schlesinger, "A Two-Dimensional Scheme for Classifying the States According to Degree of Inter-Party Competition," *American Political Science Review*, 49 (December 1955), 1120-1129.

some type of one-partyism. The data also remind us that findings vary by the office studied. Twenty-nine states were located in the same category of competition in both presidential and gubernatorial elections; the remaining 19 were located in different categories. The cate-

TABLE 1

STATE PARTY PATTERNS IN PRESIDENTIAL
AND GUBERNATORIAL ELECTIONS

Category of Inter-Party Competition	Distribution of States in Presidential Elections 1872-1948	Gubernatorial Elections 1870-1950
Continuously Competitive	9	9
Cyclically Competitive	4	4
Cyclical One-Party	16 (11 R, 5 D)	8 (5 R, 3 D)
Predominant One-Party	7 (4 R, 3 D)	16 (10 R, 6 D)
Completely One-Party	12 (2 R, 10 D)	11 (1 R, 10 D)
Total	48	48

Source: Data drawn from article cited in footnote 7.

gory of completely one-party states contained the highest proportion of states in common. On the other hand, despite the fact that 9 states were assigned to the category of continuously competitive states in both columns, only 5 of the states were the same.

Implications

Before commenting on implications of these findings, a restatement of some characteristics of this classification base will help avoid misunderstandings. The statistical complexities in working out the classification scheme should now be apparent, and these become problems because the scheme is both defined and applied in essentially statistical terms. Since studies do not agree on or validate any one "best" way to determine degree of interparty competition, they vary as to measures, categories, election districts, offices, and time periods. The differences in findings thus become in part a function not solely of the characteristics of the object studied, but also of the methodology employed. Under such conditions it cannot be too strongly stressed that the findings must be tied back to the details of the empirical investigations.

Since a belief in the efficacy of competition underlies the adoption of this classification scheme, it would be well to amplify our earlier remarks on that belief. We assume that, on the average, a vigorously competitive two-party system functions regularly more advantageously for the larger political system than an uncompetitive one-party system. This assumption is cast deliberately in terms of probabilities and not of guarantees. On occasion, close two-party competition may promote the rivalry of mediocrities or a joint deceit of the electorate, or it may direct attention to trivia, provoke excessive cleavages, and the like. At times, too, a one-party system may produce social benefits approximating those thought the province of two-partyism. Hence we stress the factor of competition neither as a panacea for party defects nor as a sufficient condition for effective party performance, but rather as necessary in most cases to maximize whatever broader usefulness the party system might have in the operation of the political system.

When party systems are classified solely by the number of seriously competitive parties in elections, the emphasis is necessarily only on quantitative relationships *between* the parties. Other aspects of party in its electing function may thereby be overlooked. For example, state party systems located within the same category of degree of interparty competition may exhibit different intraparty factional patterns.[8] Similarly, identical election outcomes assigned to the same category of interparty competition may vary in vigor and quality of campaigning, strength of party organizational effort, and how the candidates, parties, and voters perceive the degree of interparty competition. States sharing a common classification may have significantly dissimilar underlying distributions of one- and two-party local election districts. In sum, the classification scheme here endorsed is a relatively primitive taxonomic device, one which stands closer to the beginning than to the end of analysis and which requires supplementation before it discloses a full picture of party systems. Yet, allowing for these severe limitations, the findings do identify some basic elements of the party system.

American party systems are characterized by the absence of genuine multi-partyism. To a degree this finding is a product of an operational definition that accepts as an actual party only that which has

---

[8] Duane Lockard has attempted to refine a classification of state parties by use of both interparty competition and intraparty factionalism variables. See his *New England State Politics* (Princeton: Princeton University Press, 1959), pp. 324-326 and *The Politics of State and Local Government* (New York: Macmillan Company, 1963), pp. 187-189.

secured election victories or a sizable percentage of popular vote with some frequency. The resulting bias is congenial to our rough definition of party in that it permits us to exclude from the category of party so-called "third parties," which remain in politics for purposes other than to pursue power and to control government—for example the Vegetarian "party." The same bias, however, also excludes a minor party with a limited voter following that plays a continuing balance-of-power role between the major parties; or one which erupts once or twice to affect election outcomes, and is therefore unnoticed in a classification scheme geared to treat a long run of elections. Since it is preferable not to overlook such parties as integral participants in a party system, later we shall attempt to remedy this bias by briefly commenting on American third parties. For the present, the central finding remains essentially intact. The dearth of genuine multi-partyism with respect to the electing function derives primarily from the nonexistence of such multiple parties and not from the failure of our instrument to locate them.

The second major finding may surprise us, depending upon our presuppositions. American party systems are not as vigorously two-party competitive as is so often believed. In House districts for House elections, and in state presidential and gubernatorial politics, the predominant pattern clearly is one or another variant of one-partyism. Even when the nation as a whole is examined with reference to the presidency and the House, the character of the two-party competition that obtains is successive periods of one-party dominance rather than regular and frequent alternations of party control.

When reality disappoints expectations, we have the choice of deploring the reality while holding fast to the expectations, or of altering expectations and rejudging reality. Perhaps a combination of both is the most suitable reaction to this finding. Our preference for competitive two-partyism compels us to argue for considerable improvement of extant party systems. At the same time, we might rethink our notion of what we mean by interparty competition. Does effective competition really require balanced party strength and uncertain election outcomes at virtually every contest scheduled by the calendar? Or should we not build into our concept of competition a much longer time dimension so that alternation of party control at irregular intervals, coupled with the out-party's retention of significant electoral and legislative strength, would meet the test satisfactorily?

Whatever one's position on those queries, the findings plainly require us to focus on the inner politics of the dominant party as intensively as on the competition between the parties. This revised perspective comprises the essence of what Samuel Lubell has termed "a new theory of political parties." "Our political solar system . . . has been characterized," urges Lubell, "not by two equally competing suns, but by a sun and a moon. It is within the majority party that the issues of any particular period are fought out; while the minority party shines in reflected radiance of the heat thus generated."[9] Applied to the question of how adequately the party system handles its electing function, this view necessitates going behind interparty patterns to examine the nominating politics of both parties, with special attention to the majority party of the day. Similarly, while the contribution of the minority party remains critical to the effective operation of the party system, under this view its role is less as a near equal partner in government power and more as an indirect influence in its structuring the context within which the majority party exercises control.

Lubell's "sun-moon" analogy also supplies a view of third parties that supports our position. Third parties are treated as "lesser planets" which together with the Moon (the minority party) "revolve around the majority Sun. The special significance of third parties is that they shed such penetrating light on the inner torments of the majority party."[10] Examples would include the Populist, Progressive, and Dixiecrat parties, each of which represented protests against a major party based upon sectional disaffection. Since such parties deliberately attempted to alter election outcomes and to coerce the major parties into policy changes, they merit inclusion in our concept of a party system, and their activities may be evaluated as aspects of the internal politics of the major parties.

The findings on degree of interparty competition incidentally touch on some related subjects as well. For instance, there was a greater volatility in the vote for president as compared to the vote for the House. There were elements of party linkage and differentiation in voter preferences for presidential, congressional, and gubernatorial candidates. The import of these findings will be discussed later in their suitable contexts. At this point, having worked out and applied the classification scheme, it would be appropriate to test it. Specifically, since the scheme distinguishes most sharply between two- and one-party systems, are those systems really different?

---

[9] Samuel Lubell, *The Future of American Politics* (New York: Harper & Brothers, 1951), p. 200.
[10] *Ibid.*, p. 205.

Chapter II

COMPARING AMERICAN ONE-PARTY AND TWO-PARTY SYSTEMS

American political scientists, in common with virtually all other Americans, strongly endorse two-partyism as the most effective system for the United States. So deep is this conviction that as a practical matter the question may be considered closed: competitive two-partyism is the widely accepted norm for American party politics. In 1950, for example, the Committee on Political Parties (CPP) of the American Political Science Association published a major assessment of American parties, entitled *Toward a More Responsible Two-Party System*. The "two" in the title was a redundancy they could have easily dropped, since the CPP happily conceded the following point. "The two-party system is so strongly rooted in the political traditions of this country and public preference for it is so well established that consideration of other possibilities seems entirely academic. When we speak of the parties without further qualification, we mean throughout our report the two major parties."[1]

This marked preference for competitive two-partyism is accompanied, naturally, by a belief in its superiority. Two-partyism, it is said, facilitates democratic majority government, promotes greater government responsibility, makes government more sensitive and responsive to public needs and interests, and imposes greater responsibility and accountability on majority and minority parties. These judgments are, of course, relative, and the unspoken comparison is with one-party and multi-party systems. This chapter will closely examine the adequacy of these judgments with respect to one-partyism; multi-partyism will be briefly reviewed in the next chapter.

Our review of one-partyism incidentally serves another important purpose as well. The CPP *Report* is the most systematic indictment to date of the American two-party system, complemented by a full statement of proposals for its reform. Its perspective emphasizes how our actual two-party system falls short of realizing its inherent potential. In the final chapter we shall closely examine the premises, reasoning, and content of the *Report*. For the present, if we can show the inferiority of one- to two-partyism in the American context, then we are implicitly correcting the bias in the CPP's perspective. That is, whatever the deficiencies of American two-partyism compared to an idealized two-partyism, the former nonetheless performs far more effectively than American one-partyism. In the closing chapter we shall determine whether, as the CPP *Report* alleges, the glass is at least half-empty; here we seek to demonstrate that the glass is at least half-full.

That demonstration is neither as extensive nor as sure as we would like, for there are gaps in our knowledge of the operation of party systems. Paradoxically the one-party states, representing deviance from the desired norm, have received the most analytical attention. Some of our general conclusions here on the relative inadequacies of one-partyism would therefore be subject to revaluation as future studies enlarge our understanding of political behavior in competitive two-party juris-

---

[1] Committee on Political Parties of the American Political Science Association, *Toward a More Responsible Two-Party System,* Supplement to *American Political Science Review,* 44 (September 1950), p. 18. Subsequently cited as CPP *Report.*

dictions. A further complication inheres in every attempt in the social sciences to isolate the influence of any large-scale factor from other interrelated factors. There are different conditions surrounding one- and two-partyism, and differences in the operations of these party systems may partly reflect the conditions rather than the systems. These handicaps to investigation, though formidable, are not fatal. As long as we remain sensitive to both the limits and tentativeness of the findings, we can still emerge with instructive conclusions.

Minimum Characteristics of Two-Partyism

To evaluate party systems requires a basis of judgment. Perhaps we can agree on some minimum characteristics we would expect of any American competitive two-party system, and then see how one-party- ism fares in matching them. Initially we shall offer two sets of charac- teristics, though our subsequent comparisons will range wider. The unit of analysis, let us say, will be state politics.

One minimum characteristic would be the stability of voter pref- erence over time. The same two parties would contend over a series of elections, and they would monopolize most or all of the vote and elective offices. The geographic basis of each party's support from one election to the next would not differ randomly nor diverge markedly; there would be durable geographic patterns of support and opposi- tion. This stability of voter response would reflect traditional party loyalties or economic interests, or both. Without requiring either party to differentiate policy positions, we would expect at least a rough fit between the interest composition of the party's voter following and the direction of its stand on issues.

Another minimum characteristic stems from the parties' need to recruit, screen, and promote candidates for elective office. Since the parties hardly qualify as tight bureaucratic organizations, as in the structure of an army, we would not invariably anticipate that the can- didates backed by party have come up through the ranks or have demonstrated through their political record conformity to behaviors and attitudes the party deems important. It is not unusual for non- party personages such as Dwight Eisenhower and Nelson Rockefeller to start at the top. Yet in terms of probabilities most of the party's candidates for higher office would have previous political careers judged satisfactory by party criteria. Accordingly, we might expect that such party-backed candidates would respect the rules of the political game, the brokerage function of politics, and the place of party and partisanship in politics. We would also expect such candidates, in campaigning and in office, to be aware of their common membership in a collective organization known as the Democratic or Republican party, and of their ties and obligations to fellow party candidates and office holders. Making the same point negatively, we would suppose that politically ambitious persons who deviated greatly from those broad standards would have been weeded out by the party in their earlier political career and persistently denied access to higher office.

The extent to which one-partyism exhibits the two sets of characteristics just discussed will occupy much of our attention in the comparison of party systems undertaken later in this chapter. Our investigation of one-partyism concentrates mostly on parts of the South, not only because the South has provided the most durable example of large-scale, sectional one-partyism but because its politics have been subjected to more sophisticated analysis than has any other American region. Southern one-partyism further divides into multifactional and bifactional types, but before considering each separately it would be helpful to depict some contextual characteristics common to both forms of one-partyism.

General Characteristics of Southern One-Partyism

Since persistent political sectionalism can develop only when the component states maintain a high sense of unity and common purpose, our first requirement is to establish the basis of the ongoing political solidarity of the South. The "special" character of the South, in the view of both natives and outsiders, has been examined and speculated about for decades not only by social scientists but by novelists and other perceptive commentators. For all of this rich and varied probing there remains a mystique about the region that eludes full exposure, and we make no pretense here of penetrating the veil. For present purposes, fortunately, we need not push beyond citing some broad regional features that have contributed to Southern unity. These would include such items as a one-crop (mostly cotton) agrarianism, a dearth of industry and metropolitanism, low per capita income, ethnic and religious homogeneity, and an intense nativism. In addition, Southern peoples share a deeply felt special sectional history, revolving around the War Between the States and the Reconstruction period, which sustains a sense of uniqueness and separateness in their self-perceptions. Although the content of their historical attachments may be as much fancy as fact, it is no less influential in shaping attitudes and behavior.

Beyond the unifying force of these factors, there is yet an even more fundamental determinant of a common Southernism: the presence of the Negro in large numbers, and the white supremacy doctrines and patterns of behavior that have resulted. The depth of Southern solidity has derived from the region's preoccupation with the problems of race. "In its grand outlines the politics of the South," Professor Key has concluded, "revolves around the position of the Negro."[2] The present South thus evolved from the actions of the states of the defeated Confederacy (tacitly acquiesced in by the rest of the nation) in designing institutions, laws, and practices to maintain the Negro in a subordinate position. Virtually all whites accepted the legitimacy and priority of this racial goal, but whites living in areas with high proportions of Negro population (black belt whites) were specially sensitive to the race problem.

The political expression of this intense regional concern to confine the Negro to an inferior position took the form of what popularly has been termed the "Solid South." Only eleven states seceded from the Union; these same eleven states went Democratic in at least sixteen of the eighteen presidential elections from 1876-1944 inclusive. In congressional and state-local politics, the Solid South—Virginia, North Carolina, South Carolina, Georgia, Florida, Tennessee, Alabama, Mississippi, Arkansas, Louisiana, and Texas—was even more antipathetic to Republicans. Although events since 1948 demonstrate the demise of Southern one-partyism in presidential politics, the pre-1948 political description of the South as "solid" is essentially accurate.

Yet though the region was partisanly solid, to characterize the politics of the component eleven states as more or less uniform is inaccurate and superficial. The disinclination to differentiate was shattered by the publication in 1949 of Key's now classic empirical study of regional and state politics of the South.[3] The politics of the several Southern states were shown to have somewhat common basic structuring forces, but also to differ in important ways. Some states, like North Carolina and Tennessee, were much closer to a two-party

---

[2] V. O. Key, Jr., *Southern Politics* (New York: Alfred A. Knopf, 1949), p.5.
[3] *Ibid.*

situation. In Virginia and Louisiana, a durable Democratic factional machine existed. In many states for varying periods of time politics revolved around a flamboyant demagogue—Huey Long in Louisiana, "Pitchfork" Ben Tillman in South Carolina, "Tom-Tom" Heflin in Alabama, Gene Talmadge in Georgia. In Mississippi, Georgia, and Louisiana, rural-urban or hill-delta antagonisms helped shape the patterns of one-party politics. And in a few states, most notably Florida and Texas, the entry of Northern Republicans in large numbers heralded changes in partisan patterns. Southern politics, viewed internally, was not of one piece.

This study has neither the space nor the need to delineate the political patterns of each Southern state. We recognize the variety of these patterns, and we act upon that recognition in our discussion of factionalism and in our subsequent treatment of political trends in Deep South and rim South states. Against this backdrop we set forth some characteristics of one-partyism generally applicable to all Southern states that lack an effective Republican party.

In these heavily Democratic states the minority Republican party functions at best as a campaign and legislative critic to whom little attention is paid, and not as a serious contender for control of government. Until recent decades, most such Republican parties were really concerned with controlling the federal patronage available in the event of Republican capture of the White House. Accordingly, these parties wished to keep their ranks few in number, often failed to put up even token opposition to the Democrats in state-local and congressional elections, and rarely attempted to build up local party organization around the state. Given their motivation and limited concerns, a case can be made for considering these Republican parties adjuncts of national rather than of state politics. And in line with our rough definition of party, we can deny them the status of a real party. Whatever the judgment on those points, we may reasonably infer that one-party states in which the minority party has no basis of support in state politics do not have political parties in the usually understood sense.

Whether in such situations one-partyism becomes in effect no-partyism hinges on the functions performed by the majority party. But what role can the Democratic party, as party, play when the only significant political conflicts occur within the party, in contests between fellow Democrats? The broad answer is that the Democratic party has no role to play and plays no role. At times a dominant faction may take over the Democratic party apparatus as an incident of its overall control, but this seldom represents an important increment of influence.[4]

When one-party politics monopolizes, the real election outcomes take place within that party. Therefore the nomination procedures of the Democratic party must serve the functions of both party nomination procedures and of the general election in two-party areas. The direct primary is thus the nomination mechanism adopted throughout the South. Further, in keeping with the majoritarian commitment of democracy, most Southern states (nine of the eleven) require the winning candidate in the primary to have secured majority support. If that condition is not met in the first primary, then it is automatically met as a result of holding a second (or runoff) primary several weeks later at which the two leading candidates of the first primary compete.

The vigor and extent of candidate competition depend upon what patterns of rivalry obtain within the primaries of the dominant party. In contests for office, do intra-Democratic nominating politics in the primary perform as creditable a job as interparty competition in general elections? The answer is important not only as a significant characterization of one-partyism, but also to counter an otherwise mistaken impression fostered by the focus of inquiry in the next two sections of this chapter. That subsequent analysis concentrates on situations of multiple candidacies for statewide offices under two types of factional systems, and the unforewarned reader might well conclude that one-party primary elections typically involve multiple candidacies at all levels of office. We show that such is not the case by a brief but careful adaptation of a study of congressional elections and nominations, whose findings would be broadly applicable to less prestigious offices not integrated into the factional pattern prevailing in the state.

Julius Turner examined the extent of competition within the dominant party's primary in "safe" House districts for the four congressional elections from 1944-1950 inclusive.[5] "Safe" districts were defined as those in which the winner got 60 percent or more of the general election vote. Turner then investigated nominating patterns for the majority party in each safe House district to determine, among other things, the proportion of closely contested and of unopposed nomina-

---

[4] Control of the formal party organs carries with it, among other things, the power to designate nominees in the event of the death or withdrawal of a nominee or incumbent and to instruct delegates to the Democratic national convention. In recent years the latter authority has taken on political importance.

[5] Julius Turner, "Primary Elections as the Alternative to Party Competition in 'Safe' Districts," *The Journal of Politics*, 15 (1953), 197-210.

tions. A closely contested primary nomination was defined as one in which the winner had less than a two-to-one lead in popular vote over his nearest rival. By reworking some of Turner's regional data we emerge with a rather precise quantitative answer, although based on averaged data, to the question of the extent of competition in Southern primaries:

1. Of Southern House districts 94 percent were safe and 6 percent were unsafe, whereas the comparable figures for the rest of the nation were 43 percent and 57 percent. The South, with 24 percent of all districts, contained 42 percent of the national total of safe districts and only 3 percent of the national total of unsafe districts.

2. Within the category of safe districts; (a) 30 percent of Southern primaries were closely contested, compared to 17 percent for the rest of the nation; (b) 43 percent of Southern primaries were unopposed, compared to 56 percent of the rest of the nation.

These findings demonstrate that primary competition in safe House districts is more extensive in the South than in the rest of the country. The South had 42 percent of the nation's safe districts, but it had a lesser proportion (36 percent) of the nation's unopposed primaries in safe districts and a higher proportion (57 percent) of the nation's closely contested primaries in safe districts. The same findings make it clear, however, taking winning candidates from all Southern districts and from all non-Southern districts as two separate groups, that a notably smaller proportion of the former have been subjected to effective competition. About one-third of Southern but about two-thirds of non-Southern districts had close competition in either the safe-district primary or the unsafe-district general election; for the South most of that competition occurred in the former, and for the non-South in the latter. The central conclusion is, therefore, that the requirement of competitive candidacies in House contests is less well met at the primary-election stage of one-partyism than at the general-election stage of two-partyism, and the Southern findings should be comprehended within that frame. The fact, then, that Southern one-partyism performs somewhat better than non-Southern one-partyism in this respect is thoroughly overshadowed, in comparing candidate competition patterns, by the predominance of one-partyism in Southern House districts and the prevalence of two-partyism in non-Southern House districts.

Having concluded thus far that in Southern one-partyism the party organization is neutralized and typically there is less candidate competition for other than the top statewide posts than in two-party-ism, we are now ready to probe more deeply into a larger and more complex question. Does one-partyism, when it operates in a context of candidate competition, function as an effective substitute for two-partyism? We explore that problem first under multifactionalism, and then under bifactionalism.

One-Party Multifactionalism

Multifactionalism refers to the existence of three or more group-ings of politicians and supporters backing separate serious candidates in the Democratic primary, as judged by the dispersion of the vote cast in the first primary for, say, gubernatorial nominees. Key's analysis identifies Florida as the most persistent example of multifactionalism; in the four Democratic gubernatorial first primaries in Florida from 1936-1948 inclusive, for example, more than eight candidates competed and the proportion of the total primary vote gathered by the top two contenders ranged from 30 to no more than 61 percent.[6] More broadly, multifactionalism is the form of one-partyism to which all Southern one-party states belong when they are not going through a temporary period of a more structured bifactionalism.

Factions in a multifactional setting are unlike parties: they are usually transitory groupings that do not regularly reappear at each election; they lack continuity in label or name, in leadership, and in voter support. The meaning of such factions, in either personnel or policy terms, is unclear in any one election and becomes more obscure through time, bewildering the voters. The general tendency of such factions, in short, is to fail to provide guideposts for voters comparable to those supplied by parties in a two-party system.

The confusion of voters further deepens in those states where traditionally each candidate runs on his own, unaffiliated with any other candidate for another office. Suppose, for instance, that six candidates are running for governor, four for lieutenant governor, five for attorney general, three for secretary of state, two for commissioner of agriculture, and so on. If in no case a candidate for any of these posts links himself with a candidate for another of these posts, a voter want-ing to support like-minded candidates willing to cooperate with each other in office must do the best he can in constructing some sort of

---

[6] Key, *Southern Politics,* p. 89.

"slate" for his own guidance, based on whatever evidence happens to appear before or during the campaign. Thus the defects of a long ballot are compounded by the absence of any aids that simplify the voter's task by assigning identification tags to each contestant. Discontinuities of political leadership are further built into the situation by the fact that most Southern states, fearful of the emergence of statewide machines, have placed in their constitutions provisions forbidding a governor from immediately succeeding himself.

One may object that the chaos of independent candidacies is more apparent than real, if only because of the financial hardships facing every candidate in attempting to run a statewide campaign entirely on his own. The objection has some merit, but does not seriously qualify the conclusion. Deals between candidates for different posts are occasionally arranged, involving mutual support in the areas of core strength of each, by means of which each maximizes his support while minimizing cost and effort. But these deals remain known only to the professional politicians; such arrangements do not see the light of day and therefore fail to clarify candidate alignments for the ordinary voter.

Some commentators choose to describe American national twopartyism as a sham battle devoid of any meaning except that of the "ins" versus the "outs." Even if that were so, the looseness of one-party multifactionalism hinders voters from imposing even so elemental an order on the election choice. By contrast, no matter how lightly party labels may be held or how adroitly policy positions may be obscured in a given two-party state, the very existence and continuity over time of the party labels provide voters with a minimum basis for interpreting candidacies, and reduce the confusion otherwise inherent in multiple candidacies for diverse offices.

From the candidates' view, the electorate's confusion means that no candidate has a stable and persistent base from which to appeal to the voters. Yet those appeals must be made, and since the Democratic party cannot assume that role, substitutes have to be employed. The result is that the quality of campaigning and leadership under multifactionalism is likely to be inferior to that under competitive twopartyism. The evidence and reasoning underlying this conclusion repay close attention, because they involve a continuing contrast between the party systems under analysis.

In a one-party multifactional system, no ongoing party or factional organization sets the bounds within which leadership is recruited and campaigns. With the party's winnowing and screening functions unperformed, the candidacy field is wide open, both as to possible numbers and to range of quality. And each candidate is on his own in conducting a statewide campaign in a short time; no statewide party supplies him with a ready organization, policy directions, and large numbers of loyal voters. In brief, each aspirant must attempt an effective statewide appeal without having available to him the facilities routinely provided party candidates in two-party states.

Under such circumstances, a candidate may be tempted to gain notoriety on the quick and cheap by becoming what outside observers would judge a demagogue. Attention-getting stunts may appear with distressing frequency as candidates vie with each other in pursuit of the sensational, the noisy, the flamboyant. The techniques may range from the good fun of a hillbilly band to vitriolic abuse of a scapegoat, but none is likely to serve well the educative or policy function of campaigning. Similarly, the theme may vary from the sometimes innocent refighting of the War Between the States to the denunciation of Negroes, the Pope, Jews, and so on.

The pressures spurred by competitive two-partyism discourage the emergence of demagogic leaders. The party organization normally controls the ladder that the politically ambitious must climb: who gets nominated for what office, and when. In the fashion of organizations, party tends to restrict its endorsement to those who are reasonable and conformist, who know how to get along, and to cut mavericks or agitators. The party too, unlike a faction, has a past and a future, as well as a present. It therefore must consider how its conduct of a current campaign squares with its established policy positions and electoral followings and how it will affect its subsequent fortunes. Suppose that a Democratic candidate for mayor of New York City determined by simple arithmetic that he could easily muster majority election support by exploiting the resentments of whites against Negroes and Puerto Ricans. If he indulged that temptation, the Democratic party would react vigorously and adversely, and probably would repudiate his candidacy.[7] It would deliberately sacrifice its chances for the one office

---

[7] In the 1962 Democratic primary for congressman-at-large in Ohio, a segregationist candidate, unsupported by any major local party organization, won by a narrow plurality and was subsequently repudiated by the state party organization and by the Democratic governor. Though the repudiation doubtless reflected a genuine dislike of segregationist policy, it was spurred by the realistic fear that apparent Democratic endorsement of such views would hurt the chances of other Democratic candidates in the November general elections.

in order to protect both the candidacies of other Democrats for other offices in that election and the long-run future of the party itself. The party candidate, aware of his stake in the party and of the party's stake in his candidacy, thus must eschew tactics damaging to the larger organization of which he is a transient part.

Since the prevalence of demagogy is affected by a variety of forces, including the history and mores of the community itself, we argue no single-cause explanation. Rather, our position is that political structure is one of the determinants of the leadership and the character of campaigning. Judged on that basis, the political structure of one-party multifactionalism lacks the internal and external constraints characteristic of parties in a two-party system, which militate against the emergence of self-serving demagogues.

In the context of multifactional campaigning—inadequate guideposts for voters and inadequate bases of continuing support for candidates—it is not surprising that many state office contests revolve more around personalities and localism than around programs and issues. Voting patterns for candidates exhibit what Key has aptly termed the "friends and neighbors" influence: a high proportion of the candidate's total vote derives from the section of the state from which he comes, for purely local reasons unrelated to his policies or the supporters' economic interests. This tendency is not unknown to two-party systems, but the difference in degree becomes a difference in kind. Even on the level of presidential nominations the state of residence of potential candidates is a factor considered, but only as one of many items that make up presidential "availability." (Presidential election outcomes have not demonstrated the validity of this particular bit of the professional politician's conventional wisdom.) The sectional bases of two-partyism provide the effective contrast, for unlike the transient localism of multifactional bases they reflect politically relevant and durable economic or traditionalist interests. One-party multifactionalism, in brief, fails to confine the play of localism and personalism as narrowly as does a competitive two-party system.

In Chapter 1 our discussion of the key functions of parties carefully noted that democracy required the performance of these functions, and that if party failed to do so other agencies would. Providing a supply of candidates for elective offices is one of the necessary functions. The absence of party control under one-party multifactionalism creates a void in candidate recruitment and promotion, and various non-party mechanisms attempt to move into that void and handle that function. One mechanism is the potential candidates themselves, each of whom can make his own determination as to whether to run and for which office. Interest groups may put forward, in open or disguised form, one or more candidates who, if elected, will protect their interests. The influence of newspapers on election outcomes, both as to the candidate they back and the way they cover the campaign, likewise tends to be inflated because of the ambiguity and confusions of multi-factionalism. The inferiority of these alternative mechanisms to party control over candidacies needs no belaboring, and helps to support the normative position advanced earlier that parties are best equipped to perform these functions in ways beneficial to the working of democracy.

The inability of one-party multifactionalism to satisfy even the minimum expected of two-partyism in voter guidance and candidacy control does not exhaust the contrasts between the party systems. Broadly speaking, multifactionalism is less effective than party in restraining or empowering the governor, and in facilitating coordination within the executive branch or between the executive and legislative branches. Interest groups capitalize on situations of diffused power, and long-range public policy becomes difficult to formulate, legislate, or to administer.

Elective officials who have won office independently of each other, and who expect to campaign again independently of each other, have only a limited basis for mutual political coordination when in office. This difficulty is especially true for a one-term governor attempting to control his executive heads, who were elected on their own and can run for immediate re-election, and may well have an eye on the governor's office. Similarly, gubernatorial influence with the legislature is handicapped by the basic political fact that most legislators were elected for reasons unrelated to the gubernatorial contest. To the extent that governors surmount these obstacles and develop strong leadership roles—and many Southern governors have been able to do that—they must rely on exploiting their influence over patronage and pork-barrel weapons to keep legislators and administrators in line.

A Southern governor who is limited to one term, who has no responsibility to a collective political organization, and who is preoccupied with manipulating his influence resources to sustain legislative and administrative backing, has not much incentive toward long-range state planning and policy. Indeed, the temptations may run to venality in office, to the use of public office for private gain. Should a governor be inclined to take the long view, enlisting the sympathetic support of legislators would be difficult. The political structure easily permits self-seeking legislators, and invites the high influence of interest groups over legislators.

Ironically, one response to the multifactional pattern of unstable policy and lack of foresighted planning has been a movement to take certain key functions of government "out of politics," for example, placing the control of education or welfare functions under independent boards beyond the scope of the governor's administrative authority. Whatever else these "reforms" have brought about, they have also hastened the fragmentation of the executive branch by undercutting the legal authority of the governor to coordinate policy, and by hampering popular control of the policies of these virtually autonomous segments of the administration. The relative chaos of one-party multifactionalism thus speeds an attempted flight from politics.

One-Party Bifactionalism

Louisiana politics provides an excellent example of the strengths and weaknesses of one-party bifactionalism compared to the operations of competitive two-partyism.[8] Bifactionalism followed the rise to prominence and power of Huey P. Long, the Louisiana Kingfish, who became governor in 1928 and senator in 1930, and whose faction maintained itself after Long's assassination in 1935. From 1928 until very recent years the Democratic one-party politics of Louisiana has revolved around the conflict between two factions, the Longites and the anti-Longs.[9]

The durability of the bifactional structure is itself no small tribute to Huey Long's importance, and the meaningfulness of its substance further precludes dismissal of Long as just another Southern demagogue. Longism represented a pursuit of rural liberalism which linked back to the less successful lower-class protest of Populism in the late nineteenth century. There can be little doubt that Huey himself distorted that pursuit by a lust for personal power, and that the Long faction typically has pushed its liberal programs in a buccaneering,

---

[8] This section draws upon the analysis in my *Huey Long's Louisiana: State Politics, 1920-1952* (Baltimore: Johns Hopkins Press, 1956), esp. pp. 248-286.

[9] In very recent years traditional bifactionalism has been undercut by the death of Earl Long, the emergence of the race issue, and by rising Republican strength. Louisiana currently is in a transition period, a discussion of which may be found in William C. Havard, Rudolf Heberle, and Perry H. Howard, *The Louisiana Elections of 1960* (Baton Rouge: Louisiana State University Press, 1963).

highhanded, and free-spending fashion. But there also can be little doubt that Huey bequeathed to the state a well-organized politics of rational interest-voting, for a Deep South state relatively free from any distracting or sterile focus on Negrophobia.

As these judgments imply, bifactionalism far exceeds multifactionalism in exhibiting the minimum characteristics we attributed to two-partyism. The stability of the preference of Louisiana voters over time was high, each major faction drawing regularly from its own set of interests and its own geographic areas. Durable pro-Long support was centered in the uplands of northern and west-central Louisiana, populated by relatively few Negroes and by many poorer white farmers. Anti-Long sentiment was most emphatic in urban counties (New Orleans excepted), in the delta counties, and in most of the counties of the Sugar Bowl. Within the larger cities, the Long faction attracted most of the Negro vote and often the larger share of the labor vote. The policy positions of Longite and anti-Long camps matched their respective interest following, thus providing voters with a clear choice, with a politics that made sense. Louisiana factions, in brief, supplied guideposts to the electorate by continuity in name, leadership, and policy stands, and as a consequence in voter support.

Are voters in a bifactional setting as resistant as those in a two-party system to a personal leadership that undercuts basic political alignments? Suppose that in a two-party state a leader defeated in the Republican primary chose not to accept defeat and close party ranks, but rather to continue the fight by urging his Republican followers to vote for the Democratic candidate at the general election. Most of his followers and perhaps all other voters would brand that behavior a violation of the rules of the game and an affront to the integrity of the party system. Hence few voters would be expected to follow his counsel. A comparable situation under bifactionalism would arise if a leader of one faction, after being defeated in the first primary, endorsed the candidacy of a leader of the other faction before the runoff primary election. The initial question can now be rephrased more narrowly: under such circumstances, did Louisiana voters tend more to follow their factional ties or their personal leaders?

Analysis of three such instances in Louisiana during the 1940-1948 period reveals that a leader's "personal" following was not readily transferable across factional lines, and that the following was more factional than personal.[10] A political leader was assured of some sup-

---

[10] Sindler, *Huey Long's Louisiana*, pp. 265-273.

port on a "friends and neighbors" basis, regardless of his position in the bifactional structure. But such a genuine personal following was minimal because of the voters' greater concern with faction. A Longite leader from east-central Louisiana, for example, could expect a higher proportion of the Longite vote from his geographic area than another Longite candidate living elsewhere in the state; the pull of a native-son localism exists, and to a somewhat greater degree in a bifactional than in a two-party system. But if that same Longite leader ran as an anti-Long or sought to commit his following between primaries to an anti-Long candidate, most of the voters who had supported him as a Longite would not follow his factional shift, and would instead adhere consistently to their own factional commitment. The play of personal leadership is mostly confined within factional lines and neither transcends nor subverts the ongoing factional alignments. This persistent orientation of the voters toward the bifactional system, even in the face of contrary appeals by personal leaders, suggests that bifactional loyalties are effective substitutes for party loyalties in two-party states.

Louisiana voters did not restrict their cohesive bifactional behavior to gubernatorial politics. In sharp contrast to the free-wheeling individuality of candidacies in a multifactional system, Louisiana has developed an informal ticket system that links candidacies for various offices during a campaign, although the ballot contains no indication of any ticket. At the state office level, serious contenders for the nine elective posts affiliate with at least one of several state office slates, present their candidacies as a ticket unit, and identify their ticket as Longite or anti-Long. Some candidates for the state legislature and county offices may also align themselves publicly with a state ticket, if they estimate that it would aid their election chances. Voter response to the simplification of their election choices by the existence of tickets has been strongly affirmative: "In Louisiana . . . ," Key states, "the voters mark a straight ticket [for state office candidates] about as consistently as they do at a general election in a two-party state."[11] Ticket voting is most pronounced, naturally, in the runoff primary, when the number of tickets is reduced to two and overlapping tickets are at a minimum. Electoral adherence to the ticket system also means that an "independent" candidate unaffiliated with a major state ticket has slim chance to win an important state office. The ticket system within a well-structured bifactionalism thus attempts to be the functional equivalent of party slates within a two-party system.

---

[11] Key, *Southern Politics*, p. 170.

State tickets are really gubernatorial tickets because the candidate for governor both heads and dominates it. At times inferior candidates can secure state office on the coattails of the winning gubernatorial contender, but this can also occur under party slates; their common defect is presumably more than counterbalanced by the increase in voter rationality made possible by the ticket or slate device. Gubernatorial command of the ticket has its post-election counterpart in the dominance of the governor in state politics, notwithstanding the constitutional prohibition against immediate re-election. Part of the governor's political strength derives from bifactionalism and the ticket system, but part stems also from the style of leadership set by Huey and Earl Long, including their unabashed manipulation of rewards and penalties to coerce support from legislators and administrators. Whatever the relative weight of those factors, compared to multifactionalism a greater degree of coordination was imposed on the legislative and administrative branches by the executive and continuity of gubernatorial policy was more pronounced.

Two final comparisons adding to a positive appraisal of one-party bifactionalism merit mention. Party nominating procedures for governor in a two-party state by definition produce leaders of the two opposing groups who then compete for majority support from the entire electorate in the general election. The Louisiana experience has been comparable in that the gubernatorial runoff primary has regularly pitted an anti-Long against a Longite. In this sense the gubernatorial first primary determines which of the rival Longite leaders, and which of the rival anti-Long leaders, command majority allegiance within each faction. Furthermore, the strength of competition and the alternation record of Louisiana's dual factions in control of the governorship also compare favorably with that anticipated in a two-party system.

To recapitulate, the outstanding characteristics of Louisiana one-partyism have been a well-formed and enduring bifactionalism, a ticket system of allied candidacies, and a de facto centralization of political influence in the hands of the governor. Measured against one-party multifactionalism, clearly such a one-party bifactional system serves more effectively to promote the benefits associated with two-partyism. These benefits include durability of political alignments, substantive policy differentiation between factions, relative clarity of choice for the voter, minimization of localistic appeals, coordinated control of the branches of state government, and the like. The next and more demanding question shifts the focus of evaluation to the other end of the comparison. Is bifactionalism, as many Louisiana local politicians are wont to claim, "just the same damn thing" as a two-party system?[12] The answer, based on the following evidence, must be negative.

A measure of the difference between bifactional and two-party schemes is the increasing fuzziness of the former as it extends beyond the arena of state office politics. The penetration of state legislative, county, and city politics by the state ticket system is uneven and incomplete, and varies greatly with the needs of local candidates. Even when such affiliations occur, however, local contests are dominated by local matters and are not usually determined by the linkage to state tickets. As a consequence, many voters often support at the same time a state ticket and a set of local office candidates opposed to that state ticket. At the other extreme, straight ticket voting from governor down through all local offices is rare, and tends to be confined to the highly organized or bossed counties. Louisiana's congressmen operate in a similar situation; they often develop their own followings, and the voters judge them by standards independent of bifactionalism. The ticket system, in short, is functionally equivalent to the party slate only in state office posts. Otherwise, in scope, in providing voter guideposts, and in voter response to the guideposts that exist, two-partyism structures politics more effectively than does bifactionalism.

The slack in the ticket system means that neither faction has a solid political base comparable to the ward and precinct organization of parties. Although some county officials may maintain friendly ties with the Longite or anti-Long factions, these courthouse factions provide no reliable local organization for either state faction. Before each quadrennial gubernatorial primary election there tends to be a fresh scramble by state tickets for local candidate affiliation, which are determined by contemporary hardheaded assessments of relative personal gain and loss, not by pre-existing factional loyalties or organizational commitments. The limitations of the ticket system strongly suggest the improbability of any factional leader being able to build a durable state machine except by the most ruthless methods. What the popular press inflates as an awesome machine, such as that of Earl Long from 1948-1952, turns out to be rather easily defeated by a "reform" anti-Long candidate in 1952. Huey Long, on the other hand, did create a powerful state machine, but in good part through manipulating elec-

---

[12] As quoted by Key, *Southern Politics*, p. 168.

tion machinery, imposing control over local governments, and indulging in punitive legislation and actions which grossly breached democratic standards. Huey's influence also rested on an intense personification of politics and on loyalty to his person, which constitute unstable political bases more dangerous to democracy than the institutionalization of politics through party. It is doubtful if one-party bifactionalism can attain the organizational thoroughness of a two-party system without degenerating into personal or factional dictatorship.

The organizational weakness of bifactionalism is further reflected in the inability of either faction to establish stable leadership recruitment and promotion without bruising primary battles. Here again only in the heyday of the Kingfish's rule in the 1930's was the Long faction able to determine its candidate for each high office before the primary. Otherwise, the fairly constant Longite and anti-Long electoral groupings were wooed by rival intrafactional leaders. Open competition in the primaries to fix who the factional leaders really are tends to increase instability and dissension within each factional camp. For example, would-be leaders of the same faction who bitterly rail at each other during the first primary campaign often find it difficult to consolidate their forces as natural allies when faced with the straight Long/anti-Long contest in the runoff primary. This absence of a regularized path to leadership, coupled with the inability of the governor to succeed himself, also builds-in conflict within the executive branch. It became almost traditional, for instance, for Louisiana's governors and lieutenant governors to have a falling out during their term of office.

A final serious inadequacy of Louisiana's bifactionalism is that factional leaders are inconstant in their factional commitment. Our earlier analysis of the transferability of personal followings underscored the durable attachment of most voters to faction, but the analysis was made possible only because major political leaders in several instances shifted their factional identification. Seldom in a two-party system does an important Democratic or Republican figure publicly endorse and align himself with the opposition party. It is a step not lightly taken; if not irrevocable once taken, the shifter typically understands that the party he left will probably not want him back. The looseness of the bifactional system encourages factional leaders to cross factional lines more readily, with greater impunity, and with less adverse effects on their own political careers. In view of the critical importance of the behavior of leadership to the character of the political system, a serious defect of one-party bifactionalism is that loyalty to faction is less demanding and rigid than loyalty to party.

Political Coherence, Interest Advantage, and Public Policy Bias

Allowing for the divergences between its multifactional and bifactional forms, we may broadly adjudge Southern one-partyism to provide a more disorganized and discontinuous structure for politics than two-partyism. Do the deficiencies of a politics of low coherence affect all interests randomly or uniformly, or do they disadvantage certain interests disproportionately?

Voter turnout trends point the direction of the answer. Key's analysis, while uncovering greater variations within the region by state, by office, and over time than is commonly supposed, also confirmed the general impression that nonvoting rates of Southern whites were especially high.[13] In examining voting for governor, which customarily attracts the highest Southern turnout, Key found that "the turnout in the primaries almost never reaches the level of participation in general elections in two-party states."[14]

Low white turnout was accounted for in part, but only in part, by suffrage restrictions, which could be argued not to be necessary ingredients of one-partyism. Integral components of one-partyism, however, greatly shaped turnout rates as well. For example, Southern voters were deprived in two ways of the stimulus of presidential politics. The one-sided outcomes in Southern states in presidential elections depressed voter turnout and interest, and insulated the region from the attention and campaigning the major parties lavished on the politically more competitive areas of the country. And the timing of Democratic primaries was necessarily divorced from the time of presidential elections, thus further isolating the region from the excitements and alignments fostered by the latter and forcing the South to concentrate on its state-local politics more or less in a vacuum. In operating an insulated

---

[13] *Ibid.*, pp. 489-528.

[14] *Ibid.*, p. 492. This conclusion was based upon participation rates for all citizens, Negro and white, 21 years of age and over. When the measure was refined by exclusion of the Negro population the turnout level in three states was markedly higher, but the general pattern of widespread nonvoting remained true for the white South.

politics, Southern states most of the time were faced with unsatisfactory candidate competition, in the form of unopposed candidacies or of the excessive competition of multiple candidacies producing voter confusion. While as a rule opposed candidacies and uncertain election outcomes encourage turnout and unopposed candidacies do not, high voting rates are generally a function of voter perception of the relevance to the campaign of deeply felt issues, and of the efforts of political organizations, including parties, to mobilize the electorate. The de facto no-partyism of one-partyism and the neutralization of party organization precluded such electorate-arousing activities, and the overall murkiness of one-partyism impeded the ability of the electorate to make political sense of the choices before it. As Key accurately insists, "it is practically impossible under the one-party system to formulate issues and to maintain political organization that will activate the electorate to the extent that a two-party system does."[15]

Generally, when turnout levels are low, the active electorate is not a cross-section of the total citizenry. The poorer ranks of the population have the highest nonparticipation rates and are underrepresented within the voting public; the more substantial middle and upper class segments are overrepresented. This bias in the composition of the participating citizenry yields advantage to some interests, which in turn is translated, in self-perpetuating fashion, into comparable biases of public policy. The active electorate tailors public policy in its own image, and thereby further dampens the interest of the inactive segment in political affairs. Relatively few citizens possess the requisite skills, time, and other resources to manipulate a politics of low coherence, but those who do easily offset their small number by their influence over candidates and office holders. Conversely, the essential strength of the mass citizenry is numbers, but that resource can seldom be mobilized or channeled effectively without a coherent politics. The disorganized one-party politics of the South thus should be interpreted—and this is one of Key's central theses—as enhancing the power of the "haves" and the supporters of the status quo, and discriminating against the "have-nots" whose interests require alteration of the status quo. Considered historically the broad effect of one-partyism has perpetuated the antebellum regional leadership of the economically more affluent and more conservative segments of the white South at the expense of the poorly articulated needs and interests of lower-class whites and of Negroes.

---

[15] *Ibid.*, p. 523.

This evaluation is scarcely restricted, of course, to Southern one-partyism. Many middle-class reformers have pushed successfully for nonpartisan local elections. Although they would be horrified at the assertion that their reform resembles Southern one-partyism in important respects, that assertion seems sound. Allowing once again for t'·e wide variations in the practice of nonpartisan local politics and for the difficulties of isolating the effects of one institutional factor, we can ascertain some common consequences. Without the guidance and structure provided by party labels, candidates must be identified by the voters in other ways. The generally low public awareness of politics often means that a premium is placed upon the community standing of potential candidates, upon their backing by civic associations and the press, and upon the factor of incumbency. Controversial issues acknowledging intracommunity conflict tend to be avoided in favor of bland commitments to extend community progress. Candidate linkages tend to be poorly developed. The lessened clarity of nonpartisan politics promotes lower turnout, especially among self-conscious, lower-class minority groups, which find it difficult to relate their needs to the relatively formless political structure. These consequences should not surprise us, since nonpartisanship is often advanced as a way to insulate local from state and national politics and its underlying premises are hostile to parties. The nonpartisan election scheme thus resembles Southern one-partyism in exhibiting some common negations of party.

Some Institutional Limitations on the Political Coherence of Two-Partyism

The notion of political coherence can be extended well beyond the clarity of electoral choice to encompass virtually the entire government structure. Our working proposition might be that the more simplified, straightforward, and coherent the political structure of the democracy, then other things being equal, the greater the probability that a swiftly functioning majoritarian system solicitous of lower-class interests will evolve. From this view it would be difficult to design a more coherent structure than the British national government system, involving cabinet control of the legislature through the medium of the majority party. Whether the maximal political coherence of the British system provides a model worth emulating will occupy our attention in the last chapter. At this point we are concerned simply with shifting our vantage point in reviewing party systems, as we did once before when comparing bifactionalism first to multifactionalism, and then to two-partyism. Here we take another focus on one- and two-partyism: does the American institutional context common to both detract from coherence?

American political values and institutions are wedded to the concept of a diffusion of power. Separation of powers and bicameralism provide for independently elected executives and legislators with different bases of representation, require that they not be the same persons, and assign to them separate and shared powers and different terms of office. Federalism further multiplies the division of power and the number of independent offices and elections. These institutional factors taken alone (and of course they are but a fraction of what actually obtains) lower the level of coherence by making it more difficult for stable majorities either to coalesce or to exert control over numerous key points of decision making. Yet on the other hand checks and balances do satisfy important values that are less effectively served by developed structural coherence.

Assuming for the moment that the broad checks and balances scheme is an unalterable characteristic of our political structure, we can ask whether lesser institutional arrangements facilitate or impede the party's special task in America of minimizing the frictions inherent in a diffusion of power. (Recall that in Chapter I this was cited as one of the significant functions performable by the American party.) In a two-party system if one party regularly controls the legislature and the other party the executive, presumably the tensions between the two branches would be exacerbated. Logically, the capacity of party to help unify the two branches—and thus to make the political structure more coherent—requires at the very least that the same party control both branches at the same time. Let us quickly review the evidence on the point.

For 52 of the 64 years, from the 1900 elections through the 1964 elections, the presidency and both chambers of the Congress, taken together, have been either all Democratic-controlled or all Republican-controlled; divided party control has occurred for 14 years (22 percent) of that period. Of the 33 congressional elections involved, in 7 House and 5 Senate elections the out-party (the party not in control of the presidency) secured control of the respective chamber. Those 5 Senate elections occurred in 1918, 1946, 1954, 1956, and 1958; the 7 House elections included those 5 plus 1910 and 1930. The similarity of election years for both chambers indicates that an electoral tide against the in-party does not differentiate markedly from the House to the Senate. Further, all but one (1956) of those seven elections were held at midterm, at which, compared to presidential elections, the turnout is lower and somewhat differently composed. At the national level divided party control is a minority pattern, associated with the different terms of office of legislators and the president.

Comparable data for state party systems are more complex, but we may discern the main outlines from some of Key's findings.[16] Key classified 46 states according to the proportion of the 1931-1952 period when a majority of members of one or both houses of the legislature were affiliated with the party opposed to the governor.[17] In only 15 states did the same party control the governorship and both legislative chambers after each election for the full 22-year period. Fourteen of those states were thoroughly dominated by one party (the 11 states of the South, Oklahoma, New Hampshire, and Vermont); the fifteenth state was South Dakota. For our purposes the relevant states to be considered is reduced by 14, and the new total is 32. In about half of those 32 states, divided party control occurred from about one-third to two-thirds of the period. Competitive two-party states were particularly prone to divided party control, the most frequent pattern being a Democratic governor facing a Republican legislature.

These findings for competitive two-party states are to a degree explainable without referring to institutional arrangements that promote divided party control. For instance, given the condition of a close popular vote between two parties, small percentage differences in vote can easily lead to varied election results. Further, since legislators are elected by separate districts and the governor by statewide vote, different geographic distributions of the same total of popular vote can produce different legislative, but the same gubernatorial, outcomes. Finally, divided party control was associated more with Democratic than Republican governors partly because the Democrats were the minority party in most non-Southern states in the 1920's. As a minority party shifts to competitive or majority status, it initially exhibits greater electoral strength in statewide executive posts than in legislative seats.

Allowing for these influences, the major factor accounting for the

---

[16] V.O. Key, Jr., *American State Politics: An Introduction* (New York: Alfred A. Knopf, 1956), pp. 52-84.

[17] Minnesota and Nebraska, which elect their state legislators on nonpartisan ballots, were omitted.

findings remains that of a biased institutional design, namely, apportioning and districting legislative seats that favored rural areas and interests, and in light of the political alignments of the period, benefited the Republican at the expense of the Democratic party. Inequitable legislative representation can be attacked for many reasons, but our point here is simply to note how it lowers the coherence of politics in two-party states by increasing the frequency of divided party control of executive and legislative branches. State party systems are rapidly being freed of such institutional rigging of the rules of the game in the wake of the new federal judicial standards set forth in *Baker v. Carr* and succeeding cases.[18]

Party in America has the capacity also to cut vertically through the government levels of federalism to relate national and state-local politics. The timing of general elections affects this capacity greatly. Nearly half the states, in a conscious effort to insulate state from national politics, have scheduled their gubernatorial elections in nonpresidential election years. The broad effect is to decrease the chances of victory for the state party affiliated with the more popular national party, and especially to handicap the minority state party in its efforts to build up its strength. Since the fortunes of the national parties change, at least in the short run, at a rate faster than state legislatures and parties can revamp their election calendar, inadvertent self-harm can occur. Thus Republicans who shifted the gubernatorial election schedule to nonpresidential years in some states in the 1930's and 1940's subsequently were unable to take advantage of Eisenhower's phenomenal popularity in the 1950's. The same analysis applies to the relationship of state to local politics, in the timing of gubernatorial and local office elections.

The discussion in this section should remind us of some institutional impediments to political coherence in American government. Although many of these impediments exist in one-party as well as in two-party jurisdictions, their effects are especially adverse in the latter, so that in practice they lessen the performance gap between those party systems. Louisiana bifactionalism, for example, compares not too unfavorably with certain instances of divided party control in two-party situations—for example, Michigan in the 1950's, when years of conflict between the Democratic governor and the Republican legisla-

---

[18] Baker v. Carr, 369 U.S. 186 (1962), established the justiciability of legislative apportionment in conformity with the protection of the Fourteenth Amendment, and subsequent cases have elaborated the predominant standard of "one man, one vote," to which representation in both chambers must relate.

ture climaxed in a deadlock over additional taxes to offset inadequate state revenues. On the average, nonetheless, an impressive difference in effectiveness between the party systems remains, and the common American preference for two- over one-partyism appears more than justified.

Chapter III

CAUSES AND CONDITIONS OF AMERICAN PARTY SYSTEMS

The two-party system, however preferred by Americans and superior in practice to one-partyism, is not inevitable in a constitutional democracy. Investigating the causes and conditions of two-partyism in various countries doubtless would turn up many idiosyncratic factors, but common elements can be identified as well, and they may be roughly classified as institutional or noninstitutional. Since many such elements have been advanced to explain the existence of two-partyism, it would lessen confusion to set the limits of the ensuing analysis. No single-cause explanation will meet the acid test: were that factor absent or altered, would political dualism disintegrate? And of the many multiple causes advanced, the available evidence makes it difficult to establish causality as distinct from association, or to fix precisely the relative influence of each factor, especially since each not only influences but is also influenced by the ongoing party system. Accordingly, our first task in this chapter is to review and evaluate the major causes and conditions of two-partyism cited in the professional literature, with an eye to pruning the list to a "proven" combination of those that push in the same direction. Subsequently, we shall explore why the same two parties monopolize politics, and we then conclude by studying recent changes in Southern election behavior as a useful example of alterations in a party system.

Institutional Influences

It is not surprising to find, in light of the party's pursuit of power through election victory, that many analysts stress the institutional context of elections as a prime determinant of the party system. Specifically, the single-member district and plurality vote device (SMD/PV) has been held to determine two-partyism, while proportional representation (PR) based on multi-member districts has been held to produce multi-partyism. Maurice Duverger, a contemporary French analyst of comparative parties, takes this position and equates it with a law:

> . . . the simple-majority single-ballot system favours the two-party system. Of all the hypotheses that have been defined in this book, this approaches the most nearly perhaps to a true sociological law. An almost complete correlation is observable between the simple-majority single-ballot system and the two-party system: dualist countries use the simple-majority vote and simple-majority vote countries are dualist. The exceptions are very rare and can generally be explained as the result of special conditions.[1]

The SMD/PV device is usual in American election districts.[2] The

---

[1] Maurice Duverger, *Political Parties* (New York: John Wiley & Sons, 1954), p. 217. Italics in original.

[2] Exceptions include PR for local elections in a few cities, and multi-member districts in one chamber of some state legislatures and on those few occasions when all of a state's United States Representatives are elected at large. In the latter two instances, however, plurality voting is retained, and PR is not employed.

essence of the device is that the voters of a geographic area choose a single representative for a specified post, and the candidate who secures the greatest number of votes is elected. Applied to the national House of Representatives, the SMD/PV procedure would work as follows:

1. 435 separate districts within states are assigned more or less on the basis of equal population units;
2. Candidates run only for one district; votes cast in that district are not applied to any other district; only one candidate can win in that district, and hence all others lose;
3. The voter may vote only for one person for the post, and since a plurality of votes is sufficient to win, there is only a single election.

The customary contrast to the SMD/PV device is proportional representation with multi-member constituencies. The use of multi-member districts always raises the question of whether elections should be held on a winner-take-all basis or on a proportional representation basis. Under the former procedure, which obtains in the American use of multi-member districts, the party with the highest total of votes (assuming straight party voting for candidates) will send its complete ticket to office to the exclusion of all other candidates from the losing party or parties. Under the latter procedure, all parties will send representatives to office in approximate proportion to their popular strength.

Using House seats again, let us first examine the alleged effects of operating by 435 separate SMD's rather than by the whole nation as a single election district. In order to win a majority of House seats, a party must gain a plurality of votes in each of a majority of House districts. Exclusively regional parties, therefore, must content themselves with a minority of House seats, and parties with only minority followings either in few or many districts will not gain any seats. In short, a party aiming at majority control of the House must seek to be a national party.

Under the SMD plan the geographic distribution of a party's vote is as important as its absolute size. A "wastage" of votes occurs for neither the votes for the losing candidates nor those in excess of a plurality for the winning candidates are applied to other candidates of that party in other districts. This leads to what Duverger has called a mechanical and psychological polarization of parties. Since one party gains an entire House seat (100 percent) with only a plurality vote (less than 100 percent), nationally the winning party usually captures proportionately more seats for its share of the total vote than does the second-running party. The latter party, in turn, tends to monopolize the opposition because it fares proportionately better than the third-running, the fourth-running, parties, and so on. For a typical example of mechanical polarization: a party gaining 58 percent of the national popular vote wins perhaps 65 percent of House seats, the minority party gains most of the remaining popular vote but all of the remaining seats, and the other lesser parties gain no seats for their small percent of the popular vote. A psychological polarization develops when voters understand this phenomenon and are loath to waste their support on parties that have little chance of winning. Voters thus cluster around the two parties that have a practical chance of victory, thereby hastening the decline of all other parties.

In England, for example, supporters of the Liberal party know that the Conservative and Labour parties will always appeal for their votes, and that one constant theme in their appeal will be that a vote for the Liberals is a wasted vote. One response by the Liberals, quoted from a campaign flyer for the 1950 general election, testifies humorously to the minor party's difficulties in effectively rebutting this theme:

> The only wasted vote is the vote not used or the vote given to the party you do not want. If you want a Liberal but vote Tory you can't get what you want—and may not even get your Tory. If you want a Liberal and vote Liberal you may not get your Liberal—but you have had a go.

Analysts additionally hold that the plurality vote (PV) procedure also sustains two-partyism. Involving only a single election, PV may produce minority winners. Such a risk stimulates the multiple candidacies or parties that otherwise exist to enter into working alliances, to coalesce in order to strive in effect for majority vote. (We assume, of course, that the parties are not so divided by ideology that they prefer to remain apart rather than to consolidate.) The merger must take place before the election, and the most sensible division of efforts to attract a majority vote is for no more than two parties to compete. In contrast, a majority-vote requirement, in conjunction with a second or runoff election, might well encourage a multiplicity of parties to exist. Each party could run its own candidates in the first election—like factions in a one-party multifactional state—and then negotiate and make temporary alliances in the interim election period.

We should distinguish the sustenance the SMD/PV device allegedly affords the two-party system from its impact on any particular two parties. The SMD/PV device doubtless favors the incumbent major parties against challengers, but it does not guarantee their survival against a determined bid to displace them. In the United States displacement has been rapid and thorough, as exemplified by the swift disintegration of the Federalists and the Whigs in the first half of the nineteenth century. In England, by contrast, it took the Labour party several decades from its emergence in 1905 to replace the Liberal party as a major party, and the Liberals are far from defunct today.

For all its plausibility, the SMD/PV explanation of the two-party system falls considerably short of fullness and accuracy. Its chief defect is not so much that it is wrong (though it is in part) as that its scope of explanation is restricted. Duverger's "law" requires a narrowing amendment, explains less then it seems to, and must be supplemented by other factors.

Let us assume for the moment that the election scheme under analysis tends to produce a two-party system in national politics, and in the politics of each state and each locality as well. Why are the *same* two parties operative at *all* levels, rather than many different pairs of parties? Whatever the reasons—and we shall discuss them subsequently—they relate to factors other than the SMD/PV device. We can further ask why American national politics is not characterized by a sectionally based multi-partyism rather than by two-partyism. Major-party politics is often interpreted in terms of intersectional combinations and conflicts. But why should not each of the major American geographic sections have its own party instead of fighting out intersectional rivalries within the two-party structure? Certainly the mechanical effects of the SMD/PV scheme permit geographically based parties, since plurality control of a district yields control of the legislative seat of that district. Just as the election scheme handicaps a party outside its geographic areas of strength, so it enhances a party's influence within its geographic orbit. Where, then, as in the United States, sectional concerns are well developed politically and yet are not expressed in multi-party form, factors other than the election device under discussion must be influential.

The SMD/PV procedure alone similarly fails to account for the presence of local one-partyism or the absence of national one-partyism.

On the former, no election scheme can by itself create political conflict, of either two parties or many parties. The raw materials for political division must be present, and their existence or absence is independent of the election scheme. The one-partyism of Southern congressional politics, for example, co-exists without strain with the SMD/PV procedure. As to the question of national one-partyism, the election device in no way prevents a party that wins over half the national popular vote from carrying every congressional district in the nation. If the strength of the two major parties were rather evenly divided in all districts, the winning party would be assured of a near monopoly of seats in the Congress. Assuming that the same party won a long run of elections, and that it retained control of virtually all legislative seats, the losing party, even if it continued to attract high minority proportions of the popular vote, could hardly perform effectively the functions assigned to it by the two-party system. That such legislative outcomes do not occur derive from the uneven distribution of the geographic strength of the major parties. This fact, however, is independent of the election device itself; better stated, uneven geographic strength may have powerfully conditioned the acceptance of the election device. Surely the major parties and the public support the SMD/PV procedure partly because bedrock areas of backing guarantee each party a sizable fraction of legislative seats, no matter what the partisan direction of the national tide.

Duverger himself subsequently sharply confined the scope of his "law": "the true effect of the simple-majority system is limited to local bi-partism."[3] More accurately put, in the light of the preceding comments, the SMD/PV device at best helps account for the lack of multi-partyism at the local level. But whether one- or two-partyism appears at the local level, and why two parties and the same two parties control politics at higher levels, must stem from reasons other than the SMD/PV procedure.

A recent test of Duverger's hypothesis against the experience of five European nations suggests further deficiencies in this institutional explanation.[4] The study found the evidence on mechanical polarization quite mixed: there was no clear relation between the parties' proportion of national popular vote and their proportion of legislative seats captured. Other important variables included the nature and extent of malapportioned seats and the geographic distribution of each party's

---

[3] *Ibid.*, p. 223.
[4] John G. Grumm, "Theories of Electoral Systems," *Midwest Journal of Political Science*, 2 (November 1958), 357-376.

vote. The evidence on psychological polarization tended to be negative; there was little voter reluctance to "waste" votes on parties handicapped by mechanical polarization. Finally, the study underscored the fact that at times the party system shaped the election system, rather than the reverse. Thus around the turn of the century many European nations had both the SMD device and multi-partyism, a combination that produced inequitable legislative representation, consistently for some parties and arbitrarily and occasionally for others. The parties discriminated against succeeded in substituting PR for the SMD device, and thus altered the election system in order to sustain multipartyism. While these events support the broad association between election and party systems advanced by Duverger, they also remind us that the causal direction can be from party system to election device no less than its opposite, the theory ordinarily put forth.

The professional literature suggests another major institutional determinant of two-partyism—namely the popular election, as contrasted to the legislative selection, of chief executives. The reasoning is as follows. If a party wants to capture a city's mayoralty, a state's governorship, or the nation's presidency, it must in practice seek a majority of voters, and no more than two parties may compete over time with any persistent hope of success for an electoral majority. Under a parliamentary government, however, the executive is selected from the legislature by the legislators; the electorate votes only on legislators. Thus voters can indulge multi-party loyalties because a multi-party legislature can still select the executive, albeit the vigor and durability of the executive depend on the party distributions within the legislature and the party complexion of the executive.

This reasoning, while somewhat persuasive, can be interpreted to support the view that the election mechanism may be less important than the basic commitment of the electorate to a certain kind of party system or chief executive. In Britain in recent decades the Liberal party has secured a higher percent of the popular vote than of seats in Commons. The SMD/PV device has helped both to reduce Liberal strength and to stabilize it at a low level. At times, such as that following the Labour victory in 1964, the close balance between the major parties may give the Liberals a strategic strength well beyond its number of seats. To the extent that the durability of the Liberals may be credited to the parliamentary form of government it supports the influence on the party system of the mode of choosing the executive. But surely the overriding characteristic of British national politics, allowing for the special niche of the Liberals, is two-partyism? And could it not be suggested that the preference of most Britons for a stable and effective government commits them to a two-party politics in spite of the opportunities for multi-partyism inherent in the parliamentary form?

Much the same argument could be applied to the American experience. The president is of course elected not by direct popular vote, but indirectly through the unique Electoral College device. In the event no candidate secures a majority of the electoral votes, the Constitution specifies procedures for congressional selection from among the top three contenders. If the major geographical sections of this nation had developed a multi-party system that included regional candidates for the presidency, our election arrangements would have assured the eventual emergence of a president, even if one selected by the Congress. Yet the American people are markedly averse to taking advantage of the opportunities for multi-partyism logically inferable from this provision for contingent legislative selection. Instead, they have clearly preferred to determine presidential contests by action of the Electoral College, that is, by their own popular vote as distorted by the federalistic and other biases associated with the Electoral College procedure. Could not this pattern also be considered an outgrowth of popular commitment to have as presidents only those who have majority voter backing, a commitment comparable to the British preference for stable executives? We may conclude, therefore, that while the method of electing the chief executive does influence the number of parties in the party system, other noninstitutional factors may well be more determinative of two-partyism.

Noninstitutional Influences

Some writers advocate the "naturalness" of the two-party system on the grounds that rational political choice follows a dualistic "for or against," and from this they deduce a tendency toward a division into two parties. Duverger is of this view: ". . . the two-party system seems to correspond to the nature of things, that is to say that political choice usually takes the form of a choice between two alternatives. A duality of parties does not always exist, but almost always there is a duality of tendencies."[5] This perspective may reflect the penchant of the Western mind for dichotomies; we could argue as persuasively that a threefold division is natural, namely, Left, Right, and Center. Since most com-

---

[5] Duverger, *Political Parties*, p. 215.

munities resolve many more than one issue at a time there is no reason why the alleged tendency to dualistic choice on each single issue should aggregate neatly to sustain two- rather than multi-partyism. Duverger himself, as we shall see, shrewdly cites the existence of a "conflict of conflicts" as a major reason for French multi-partyism.

If a dualistic division is not natural to human beings in general, then perhaps it is to certain segments identifiable by personality, temperament, or culture? One chauvinistic answer would seek to relate two-partyism causally to "Anglo-Saxon political maturity" and its absence to "the temperament of the Latin races." There may well be some merit in associating the character of parties and politics with national temperaments, especially when stressing the influence of cultural factors and pervasive political values, but the preceding parochial formulation is simply too slippery to encourage credence. Again, while the relevance of personality type to political behavior seems reasonable, we as yet lack the detailed knowledge connecting the two which would permit us to include this factor.

Other analysts proffer the logically more attractive explanation that the American party system is dualistic because it happened to be dualistic at its inception. Unfortunately, these analysts differ on which sets of dualisms were controlling: the English heritage of Whig and Tory, ratification versus rejection of the new Constitution, federal versus confederate nature of the new Union, agrarian versus mercantile-business interests, coastal versus inland interests, etc. The disagreement should not obscure the insight in attempting to locate the explanation in the history of the party system. Since any party system has impressive momentum and staying power because of certain sociological processes, an effective accounting of its origins would also help explain its later shape.

Probably the most fruitful noninstitutional explanation of the number of parties composing the party system relates broadly to the character of social conflict and consensus in the nation. At bottom, no party system can be viable unless all important interests in the nation respect political disagreement. This respect presupposes a developed sense of national identity and community and widespread agreement on which political methods are and are not legitimate or acceptable. If a major party were dedicated to a basic change in the regime no two-party system could operate, and the presence of such a party in a multi-party setting, even if it were carefully isolated from sharing in power, would complicate the workings of government. Assuming there exists a social consensus which legitimates disagreement and the ways it is expressed politically, the depth and congruence of the existing social cleavages heavily influence what the number of parties will be.

Where, for example, divergences of opinion are both intense and noncongruent, the raw materials for an unstable multi-partyism are present. Such has been the case with France, as Duverger has noted.[6] A two-party system could have formed in France on the clerical/anticlerical issue, on free enterprise/planning, or on East/West in the Cold War. The noncongruence of these cleavages, however, multiplied the number of parties and precluded durable alliances covering the whole spectrum of policy. Communists and Socialists, for instance, diverged on the Cold War controversy though they could ally on the other two conflicts; "Progressive Christians" could side with the Communists on two of the basic issues, but not on the clerical/anticlerical dispute.

When a conflict of conflicts such as that which obtains in France is absent, maintaining a stable two-party system is facilitated but not guaranteed. There are, after all, election areas so dominated by one economic concern or so homogeneous in their political interests that they cannot generate enough conflict to support two-partyism—the South's involvement with the race problem, for example. And on the other hand, a single cleavage may at times provoke an intensity of feeling capable of pulling apart the two-party system and the nation, as in the Civil War. The continuance of stable and moderate two-party systems depends, then, upon a happy balance struck between consensus and conflict.

For most of its history the United States has apparently been able to keep that balance. Political conflict based on diverse interests takes place within the limits of a broad agreement on political democracy, economic enterprise, the primacy of the individual, material progress, social mobility, and the like. Even when suppressed minorities such as the Negro undertake to act collectively to advance their position, they define their wants in terms of the traditional goals of the society. So circumscribed, political conflict tends to be restricted to secondary goals or to means of realizing widely shared primary goals. The setting of economic expansion further serves to lessen the stakes and the bitterness often associated with struggles of economic interests. Then, too, federalism has left the resolution of many provocative issues to the states and localities, while the First Amendment tradition has kept

---

[6] *Ibid.*, pp. 231-233.

explosive religious controversies from embittering national politics. Finally, the nonideological cast of voters and major parties alike perpetuates a low-key style of politics that favors compromise and discourages the extremism of conflicts fought out in the name of high and unnegotiable principles. The American national experience has sufficient conflict to maintain two- rather than one-partyism, and sufficient consensus to avoid fractious multi-partyism and to sustain a moderate rather than immoderate two-partyism.

Notwithstanding the plausibility of the preceding explanations, it still remains something of a mystery why or how the American people have been able to maintain a balance of conflict and consensus promoting conciliatory two-partyism. Allowing for our inability to uncover these "ultimate" determinants, probably the mix of consensus and conflict in the society influences the number of parties more than do institutional devices. Yet institutional arrangements, even if secondary in effect, also shape the party system; and both categories complement rather than compete in their effects. The durability of our party system can be credited not only to the institutional and noninstitutional factors we have discussed, but to the capacity of any party system to mold the views of rising generations on its own behalf.

Why the Same Two Parties Monopolize American Politics

Our conception of two-partyism clearly presumes that the same two parties operate at all political levels, as distinct from the logical alternative of different sets of two parties competing in different political jurisdictions. Yet the discussion thus far has not directly confronted the question of why the former situation exists rather than the latter. The scope of Duverger's "law," it will be recalled, was confined to the local level, and hence was unable to answer the question here raised. In this section we treat several factors which in combination seem to do so.

American major parties obviously need state party affiliates. The basic unit in presidential and congressional elections is the state and the national party is in many ways a loose coalition of state parties. Hence the national parties require state and local operations of some stability and durability, a need best met by units that bear the same label as the national parties themselves. But the organizational requirements of the national parties provide at most only half the answer to the question we have posed, because we then must explain why the citizenry has responded to those affiliate organizations to conduct their state-local politics.

The answer is essentially pragmatic: most voters do not sharply differentiate between state and national politics. Election statistics reveal gross parallels in the voting for presidential and congressional candidates, for presidential and gubernatorial candidates, and even for congressional and gubernatorial candidates. When a state or region shifts in party support, all three levels of elections tend to shift in the same direction, and not infrequently by roughly the same magnitude. The congruence of party outcomes across a range of political offices is greater, naturally, when the elections for those offices are held at the same time.[7] These parallels derive primarily from the extension to state-local politics of the voters' commitments in presidential politics.

Voter preferences in local, state, and national politics reveal gross parallels, not precise correspondences. The national parties are not so tightly integrated to compel their state and local affiliates to offer equal support to all party candidates at all levels. When a presidential candidate is unpopular in a state, the affiliated state party will often soft-pedal the presidential race and concentrate on its own elections. And some voters do consciously deviate from a single party preference in a range of office contests. Party outcomes may thereby be affected, especially in competitive two-party jurisdictions where small differences in voter support can determine victory or defeat. Then, too, a uniform partisan trend at all political levels may result from outside factors common to all rather than to the downward push of national political alignments. Finally, recall the findings on classifying party systems in Chapter I, particularly the fact that more than a few states were classified differently for presidential compared to gubernatorial politics.

Bearing in mind the significant qualifications and limitations just cited, we may nonetheless reaffirm the soundness of several general conclusions. Voter preferences in national and state politics do tend toward congruent support for candidates of the same party in different levels of office. The congruence is due mostly to the penetration of state-local politics by presidential loyalties or by party loyalties fixed by national politics. These conclusions suggest the broad proposition that the national parties in effect determine which state parties are able to contest seriously through time for state offices. Restated more moder-

---

[7] We noted toward the close of Chapter II that one way to increase the separation of state from national politics was to maintain different election calendars; divided party control of the presidency and the Congress is an outgrowth mostly of midterm elections.

ately and precisely, this proposition merits testing: state parties organized solely to control state government and unaffiliated with either national major party should seldom exist, should only rarely gain power when they do exist, and should soon dissolve or fuse into the ongoing two-party system if they do gain power. The record supports the first two assertions; to examine the third, we will briefly review the fortunes of the Nonpartisan League of North Dakota and the Liberal party of New York.

The Nonpartisan League (NPL), one of the most durable political expressions of Western radical agrarianism, played a central role in North Dakota politics and was important in several other states as well.[8] It arose as a farmer protest against the domination of the state Republican party—North Dakota being a predominantly Republican state—by grain and railroad interests. Its main political weapon was the direct primary mode of nomination, a reform adopted during the 1906-1912 administration of Governor John Burke, who was elected by the coalition support of "progressive Republicans" and Democrats. The stance and tactics of the NPL are revealed in the argument advanced by Arthur C. Townley, founder and leader of the NPL in its formative years. Townley urged that the state Republican and Democratic parties, unlike their counterparts in national politics, were not different in their policies; both state parties were the agents of business interests that exploited the farmers. The problems of state politics, however, were separable from national politics, and were more relevant to farmer needs. In state politics, therefore, farmers must cease being divided by the meaningless artificiality of Democratic and Republican labels and, through cohesion and tight organization, become a new and controlling political group that would support any candidate of any party who was favorable to farmer demands as defined by the platform of the NPL.

The essential NPL tactic was to enter the primaries of the existing parties to nominate candidates pledged to support of the NPL program, and then to back those candidates, regardless of party, at the general election. Often the NPL created candidates by its endorsements, in effect acting as a non-party preprimary force to raid and control the party primary. Since North Dakota was Republican, the

---

[8] This section on the NPL draws heavily on the following sources: Robert L. Morlan, *Political Prairie Fire: The Nonpartisan League, 1915-1922* (Minneapolis: University of Minnesota Press, 1955); Samuel P. Huntington, "The Election Tactics of the NPL," *Mississippi Valley Historical Review*, 36 (March 1950), 613-632; and Samuel Lubell, *The Future of American Politics* (New York: Harper & Brothers, 1951), esp. Ch. 7, "The Myth of Isolationism."

Republican party was the principal arena of conflict; the NPL also endorsed Democrats however, in keeping with its indifference to party labels. The NPL did not necessarily respect the finality of a party's primary; if it lost it frequently ran its defeated candidate as an independent or supported the other party's candidate in the general election. By skillful use of these tactics the NPL secured control of the state government in its first two years of effort, 1916 and 1918. In the latter year, anti-NPL forces created the Independent Voters Association (IVA), which by attempting to emulate NPL tactics accelerated the obliteration of the firm two-party lines begun by the NPL.

By the early 1920's, the NPL's attempt to become a national agrarian power had collapsed and its regional strength become less cohesive, varying with the political configuration of each state. In North Dakota under William Langer the NPL continued as a disciplined faction within the Republican party, often capturing state and congressional posts. Its opposing faction was the Republican Organizing Committee (ROC), the more conservative wing that succeeded the IVA. In 1956 the NPL convention entered its candidates for state office in the Democratic party, and in 1958 the NPL merged with the Democrats and left the Republican party to its conservative rivals. The merged group elected Quentin Burdick in 1958 as the first Democratic United States Representative from North Dakota, and Burdick then captured the Senate seat made vacant by Langer's death in 1959. By late 1964, the Democrats had amassed sufficient strength to control, for the first time in the seventy-five years of North Dakota's statehood, one house of the legislature.

The NPL evolution is striking evidence of the capacity of the two major parties to monopolize effectively the two-party system in both resisting the development of a persistent third party, and resisting displacement by a new major party within the continuing two-party system. In addition, the NPL developments confirm the thesis that the attempt to maintain a political force in state politics, unrelated to nor cut across by national political alignments, tends to produce tensions that are resolved in a greater articulation of state and national political alignments.

Separate third-party activity, which constitutes a frontal attack on the two-party system, was seldom indulged in by the NPL, and met mostly with election failure. Its only important success was the capture of Minnesota's two Senate posts by the Farmer-Labor party. The NPL often attempted, however, a truncated version of third-party activity by competing anew in the general election for the offices it had lost in the preceding primary fight within the dominant party. The generally failing quality of this tactic testified to the overriding pull of the existing two-party system, as exemplified by North Dakota events in 1920. In the Republican primaries that year, NPL-backed candidates won nominations to five of ten state posts, and IVA-endorsed candidates gained the nomination for the remaining five posts. In the general election, the NPL entered a new independent candidate for each of the five positions it had lost in the primary, while the IVA endorsed Democratic candidates for the five posts it had lost in the preceding Republican primary. The outcome was a dramatic triumph for party regularity: not only did the entire Republican ticket win, but each winner had about the same vote margin, whether backed by the IVA or the NPL.

The NPL's most common and effective election method was an "infiltration and takeover" of the nominating processes of the majority party by exploiting the direct primary. Then in the general election the NPL endorsee who had won the party nomination would benefit from the support of loyal party voters (including those within the NPL's own ranks), plus that of NPL farmers normally attached to the minority party yet willing to cross party lines. The heavy reliance on this method by the NPL, together with the fact that it produced most election victories, provides lessons applicable to the question of the monopoly of politics by the same two parties.

Townley's concept of a nonpartisan, cohesive farmer bloc could have been implemented either within or outside the two-party system. The NPL chose to operate within the existing two-partyism, albeit to exploit one or both of the major parties. The NPL used the two parties to get its candidates into public office, remaining profoundly indifferent to and cynical about the party qua party. The NPL logically could urge its supporters in the minority party to raid the open primary of the majority party to help produce an NPL nominee, and subsequently could refuse to abide by the finality of the primary by continuing the contest into the general election. No matter how manipulative its approach to the parties, the NPL tacitly acknowledged the staying power and resistance capacity of the two-party system and of the Democratic and Republican parties by its central reliance on an "infiltration and takeover" tactic.

Moreover, the later development of the NPL underlines the absorptive capacity of the two-party system. Townley may have hoped initially to develop a free-wheeling agrarian bloc maneuvering within and between both major parties, but he soon found that political success was confined largely to the majority party's primary. The NPL rapidly became a disciplined faction within the majority party of the state, distinguished by occasionally allying with the minority party in the general electon. The NPL's inability to buck the two-party system as a truly nonpartisan force exhibits characteristic American political behavior that greatly supports two-partyism and the ongoing durability of the component major parties. Political dissidence tends to work itself out within the favored major party, sometimes in a massive electoral shift from majority to minority party, and only rarely in the establishment of third parties.

The ultimate disintegration of the NPL and its merger in the late 1950's with the Democrats furnishes some additional evidence on the question under examination. Because of the farm policy stands of the national parties, many NPL members were increasingly attracted to the Democratic party during the 1920's and 1930's; yet in state politics they continued to operate as a Republican faction. Whether the tensions inherent in such divergent partisan attachments would ultimately have provoked a realignment unfortunately cannot be determined. Another factor intruded, the effect on which was to hasten the break-up of the NPL and of comparable radical agrarian groups elsewhere. That factor was the development of isolationist attitudes in foreign policy, linked in good part to the German origin of many NPL members. Those who were motivated largely by such ethnic concerns turned to the national Republican party or to short-lived third-parties, such as Father Coughlin's Union party, which ran the veteran NPL leader William Lemke for president in 1936. Those oriented primarily to economic liberalism remained attracted to the national Democrats. The resultant tensions split agrarian radicalism: the Farmer-Labor party in Minnesota merged with the Democrats, the Wisconsin Progressives re-entered Republicanism as a conservative force, and the North Dakota NPL eventually merged with the Democrats. Instructively, it was the older generation of NPL members, who were most resentful of the national Democrats on ethnic-isolationist grounds, who resisted merger with the state Democrats and ultimately remained with the state Republican party. Allowing for the special role of this ethnic-isolationist factor, we may still fairly conclude that the demise of the NPL and the eventual closer articulation of state and national political alignments in North Dakota testify to the structuring force of national on state politics.

At first blush the durability of the Liberal party of New York seems to require a major amendment of our thesis, but further analysis reduces its force to a refining footnote. The Liberal party was an offshoot in the early 1940's of the American Labor Party (ALP), which was formed in 1936 to support Franklin D. Roosevelt without supporting Tammany Hall. While the ALP dissolved in 1956, the Liberal party continues to be important in the city and state politics of New York.

Several advantageous circumstances fully account for the vitality of the Liberal party. As a third-party movement, it has exploited a tight balance-of-power situation between the major parties in state politics, and often in New York City politics as well. (The certain control of the important city-wide offices by the regular Democratic organization is more popular myth than reality.) The Liberal party has been the vehicle of trade union leaders and educators, none of whom has depended on politics for a living or has required frequent election victory for personal survival. This leadership, together with trade union financing of party activity, has enabled the Liberal party to pursue liberal policy goals in politics without requiring high election success in its own candidacies. Finally, and perhaps most importantly, the Liberal party thrives on an unusual state election law. In most states, if a third party wishes to support a major-party candidate, the followers of that third party have to vote for that candidate on the major party's ticket on the ballot. Hence the contribution of the third party to the total vote of its endorsee is seldom clear, and if that practice becomes habitual, the third party is likely to disintegrate. Under New York law, a candidate may be the nominee of two or more parties, and his name is listed on the ballot under each of the parties nominating him. Votes cast for him on the minor-party ballot are tallied separately, and are of course added to those cast for him on the major-party line. This procedure permits the third party to pinpoint its effect on election outcomes, so that if it can manage to hold a balance-of-power position its influence will far exceed its numerical strength. In essence, this is what the Liberal party has done.

The ostensible goals of the Liberal party are to persuade both major parties to adopt more liberal policies and present highly qualified candidates. The lever of persuasion is the large bloc of Liberal party followers, allegedly capable of shifting their support from one election to the next between the major parties, and even of backing their own third-party candidates. Actually, the Liberal party is not a free-wheeling third force; it is so closely attached to the Democratic party that its maneuverability is confined by its reluctance to punish the Democrats by helping Republicans win office. At the Democratic state convention in 1958 Carmine DeSapio, head of Tammany Hall, thwarted the wishes of Mayor Robert Wagner and Governor Averell Harriman by leading the New York City delegates to support Frank Hogan's nomination for United States Senator. At the ensuing Liberal party convention, agonized argument and counter-argument consumed days. The boss-led Democratic convention had come up with a candidate unattractive to the Liberal party, precisely the sort of situation inviting Liberal party retaliation. On the other hand, the Liberal party leaders did not care to help the election chances of Kenneth Keating, the Republican candidate. Ultimately they decided to back Hogan, but Keating won in the general election.

The Liberal party clearly has not been able to escape the dominating pull of the existing two-party system. Less an independent third party than an occasionally defecting satellite of the Democrats, its flexibility is circumscribed by its partisan attachment. The experience of the Liberal party is merely a small qualification of the thesis that the major parties are capable of absorbing or discouraging state parties that attempt to function as an independent or challenging third force.[9] The validation of that thesis goes a long way to answer the question of why the same two parties monopolize politics at all levels.

Changes in Party Systems: The Example of the South

A review of partisan shifts in the South in recent decades provides further insight into the causes and conditions of party systems.[10] You will recall from Chapter II that the region was long characterized as the "Solid South" because its attachment to the Democratic party was

---

[9] Liberal party support in 1965 of Republican John Lindsay's New York City mayoralty bid on a fusion ticket was motivated in part by the leadership's desire to establish greater independence from the Democratic party. Immediately following Lindsay's victory, Liberal spokesmen asserted that the Democrats could not count on automatic Liberal support in the future. Even if the Liberals succeed in developing a more independent stance, their continued existence remains explainable in terms wholly within the rationale of the two-party system.

[10] I have commented more fully on these developments in "The Unsolid South: A Challenge to the Democratic National Party," in Alan F. Westin (ed.), The Uses of Power (New York: Harcourt, Brace & World, 1962), 229-283, esp. 278-281; "Editor's Epilogue: Some Trends, Judgments, and Questions," in Allan P. Sindler (ed.), Change in the Contemporary South (Durham: Duke University Press, 1963), 223-238; "The South in Political Transition," in John C. McKinney and Edgar T. Thompson (eds.), The South in Continuity and Change (Durham: Duke University Press, 1965), 298-321.

intense in presidential politics and even more pronounced in state and local politics. In terms of the propositions argued in the preceding section, Southern one-partyism was just another example of congruent electoral alignments on all levels of political office. In the last twenty years, however, the South's one-partyism in presidential politics has eroded, and electoral realignments may also be taking place more slowly in sub-presidential politics. These changes repay close study for they allow us better to understand not only the South but important factors determining the shape of the party system as well.

When the Democrats displaced the Republicans as the predominant national party, their new allies and policies inevitably strained the marriage between the South and the national Democratic party. The defection of rim-South states from Al Smith in 1928 suggested these tensions, but events after 1932 account for the contemporary Southern rebellion against the Democrats, which involves the states of the Deep South no less than the rim South. Table 2 sets forth the instances of defection; in recent elections presidential Republicanism has increased

TABLE 2

NON-DEMOCRAT VICTORIES IN SOUTHERN STATES,
PRESIDENTIAL ELECTIONS OF 1928, 1948-1964

States	1928	1948	1952	1956	1960	1964
Arkansas						
North Carolina	R					
Georgia						R
South Carolina		SR				R
Mississippi		SR			U	R
Alabama		SR			½U	R
Louisiana		SR		R		R
Texas	R		R	R		
Virginia	R		R	R	R	
Tennessee	R		R	R	R	
Florida	R		R	R	R	

R—Republican. SR—States' Rights (Dixiecrat). U—Unpledged or "free" electors, who voted for Senator Harry F. Byrd (Dem., Va.).

notably in all Southern states, including those in which electoral votes continued to be cast for the Democratic ticket.

Even a casual inspection of Table 2 affirms that the South has been irregular in its defection patterns, as to which states defected when and to what alternative party. Gauging the durability of defection is further complicated by the transient special character of each presidential election from 1948 on: white anxieties about the race issue in 1948 and 1964, the Republican candidacy of a vastly popular war hero in 1952 and 1956, and the Democratic candidacy of a Catholic in 1960. Bearing these complications in mind, we here restrict comment to the larger directions of political change.

Southern disaffection with the presidential wing of the national Democrats broadly reflects the economic conservatism or the racial fears of whites, or a combination of both easy to come by—federal protection of Negro rights necessarily involves extending national government authority and, in the view of some white Southerners, abridging private rights. Although it would be misleadingly simple to attribute the rim-South's turn from the Democrats to economic motives, and that of the Deep South to race concerns, the distinction between the two motivations provides a useful way to organize a discussion of regional political change.

The race issue, which heavily colored Southern electoral response in 1948 and 1964, and somewhat less in 1960, is so crucial to some states that given the chance it could well alter major-party alignments. Any analyst's prediction of future Southern political behavior turns on whether the South will be given that chance. It is doubtful whether either major party could afford to take a position on the Negro pleasing enough to the Deep South without thereby alienating voter support elsewhere in the country, not to mention the rising Negro vote in the South itself. In the not distant future, then, white Southerners with intense race feelings will not be able to choose between the major parties on that basis, and in that sense the race issue will be more or less neutralized politically.

The Deep South's racial stance indexes its increasing isolation from the nation on the Negro question. Any persistent Southern pursuit of a race-based politics in presidential elections will likely channel into extremist third-party activity seeking to exploit the Electoral College procedure, probably by attempting to deprive the major-party candidates of the requisite majority of electoral votes and throwing the election to the House of Representatives. This tactic, which underlay the defections of 1948 and 1960, is one of desperation, befitting the intransigence of the Deep South on the race issue. While the American political system permits the eruption of third-party movements, it profoundly discourages their stability over the long pull. Hence there can be no long-range future to this strategy of extreme disaffection, however comforting it may presently be as cathartic expressions of the Negrophobia of whites. The Deep South must ultimately acquiesce in the predominant national position on the race issue, and it must ultimately return to making its presidential choices within the bounds of the existing two-party system. When this happens, we can expect Deep South whites to divide their votes between major-party aspirants for the same reasons motivating other Americans around the country.

In contrast, economic-induced defection from Democratic presidential candidates is both more durable and more predictable in direction. The increasing dissatisfaction of Southern economic conservatives with the new policies of the national Democrats was evident during Roosevelt's administrations, but it did not erupt into large-scale defection until the favorable circumstances of 1948. Truman was a more vulnerable target than FDR had ever been, and the race fears of the region, exploited skillfully by leaders as concerned with economic as with race matters, were aroused by Truman's endorsement of a federal civil rights program. Initially expressed in the third-party movement of the Dixiecrats in 1948, this economic component of party defection increasingly took the form of presidential Republicanism. The new strength of presidential Republicanism is not uniform, of course, throughout the region: it is stronger in the urbanized, industrialized, and retirement areas, and in the rim-South states two-party competition in presidential politics is now standard. This trend, the passing of the Solid South, can only be sustained and enlarged as the South advances and diversifies economically.

The current political transition of the South is an example of large-scale shifting in party strength and party systems. Freed from an attachment to the Democratic party based on race needs, certain regional interests turned to more "natural" political alternatives. The demise of the Solid South and the rejuvenation of presidential Republicanism reflect the South's gradual return to the political mainstream of the nation. But this return is mostly on the level of presidential politics. As a consequence, Southern defection has aggravated important problems of intraparty relationships for the national Democrats. The problem of the mutual obligations and ties between state parties and the national party receives attention in the next chapter. At this point, we concentrate on the co-existence of presidential Republicanism with continued Democratic control over state-local politics. This is a question of the relation of state and national parties and political alignments, a problem we discussed earlier in examining the Nonpartisan League and the Liberal party.

The new vigor of presidential Republicanism will carry over to Republican congressional and state-local politics in the South. As ambitious leaders emerge and regularly contest for more offices, the vitality of party organization and electoral support for sub-presidential Republican nominees will increase. But contrary to what many commentators suggest, it is neither inevitable nor even probable that the strength of sub-presidential Republicanism will approach that of presidential Republicanism in the near future. The economic dissatisfactions spurring presidential Republicanism do not find in sub-presidential politics a corresponding incentive to defect from the Democratic party. Were the dominant Democratic factions in state-local politics liberal, or were most Southern Democratic congressmen liberals, regional conservatives might transfer their affections to state Republicanism. But manifestly such is not the case nor does it threaten to be. Conservatives combine loyalty to the Democratic party at sub-presidential levels with desertion from it in presidential contests. This hybrid voting behavior may be called "Republicrat," and obviously it must depress Republicanism in Southern congressional, state, and local politics.

The congruence of sub-presidential and presidential alignments turns, therefore, on compelling Republicrats to give up their partisan straddle and attach to a single party, either fully Republican or fully Democratic. With no effective sanction over rank-and-file voters, little can be done to alter their Republicrat behavior. But at least in theory the Democratic party can pressure their party and government leaders who are prone to defect, and these leaders are crucial to the development rate of Republicanism at both presidential and sub-presidential levels. Suppose that Southern Democratic leaders who wanted to support Republican presidential nominees publicly knew that such action could lead the national convention to refuse to seat their delegation, or the presidential wing to back a rival "loyalist" faction in the state, or the president to block patronage to the dissident group, or the congressional party to oust defectors from key committee posts within the chamber. What would the Southern leaders' reactions be under such circumstances?

The capacity of a major party to impose sanctions is treated in the next chapter. For present purposes, we need suggest only the following argument. If the chances of invoking such retaliatory sanctions were slim, then most such Democratic leaders could continue as Republicrats, assuming rank-and-file support in the state, with relative impunity. If, however, retaliation was probable, the would-be defectors would have to forego their Republicrat stance and take on the same party coloration for all levels of elections. For which party would most of these leaders then opt? In view of the benefits to a Southerner of retaining the Democratic label in sub-presidential politics, most leaders would reassume full Democratic identification. One supporting clue is that the leading Republicrats tend to be state and local Democrats, not Democratic congressmen.

Somewhat ironically, then, we may conclude that while Republicrat positions maintained by Democratic leaders impede the development of sub-presidential Republicanism, efforts to coerce these leaders into a consistent partisanship will probably strengthen their Democratic affiliation, thus reducing Southern Republican strength at *both* presidential and sub-presidential levels. Only if it were no longer advantageous to a conservative Southern congressman or state leader to hold on to the Democratic label would he move in the direction of Republican affiliation. The loss of advantage would lie in the stable control of state politics by liberal Democratic factions or a general displacement of conservative Democrats from strategic posts of congressional power. Without these conditions, the Republicrat phenomenon—meaning the coexistence of a reasonably competitive two-partyism in presidential politics with a predominant Democratic one-partyism in state-local politics—could exhibit impressive staying power for the foreseeable future.

If the Republicrat pattern did prove durable we might have to qualify the conclusions we have reached on the instability of conducting state politics on alignments divorced from national politics. The situations, to be sure, are not equivalent: the noncongruent alignments in the South stem from the different appeal of the major parties at presidential and sub-presidential levels, whereas the Nonpartisan League and the Liberal party illustrate attempts to promote separatist politics unaligned with the national parties to conduct state-local politics. Still, the generalized lessons drawn from our consideration of the latter two groups should be broadly applicable to the Southern experience. Assuming that our analysis imposes the obligation of prediction, we would expect that over the long pull the tensions inherent in the Southern Republicrat position would compel its abandonment in favor of more congruent party alignments in national and state-local politics.

Chapter IV

SOME GENERAL CHARACTERISTICS OF AMERICAN NATIONAL PARTIES

The conventional depiction of the major American parties emphasizes their confederate structure, their indifference to ideology, their lack of policy distinctiveness, and their limited influence in the legislature and the electorate. A fuller account of the nature and role of American national parties requires some revision of these perspectives and evaluations. We shall thus examine the centralizing forces of inner party structure, and reassess the influence of party on legislative outcomes and voter decisions. By analyzing those topics, we also hope to provide some basis for appraising the strengths and weaknesses of the American party sytem, a theme which is the focus of the concluding chapter.

Decentralization

American national parties are more national in name than in fact. Party control tends to be decentralized, and much of what passes for national politics and national party activity is persistently localistic. State and local parties comprise the influential units of the national party, and the collaboration of those parties gives life and visibility to the national party in presidential-election years. State legislation regulates the existence and the detailed conduct of political parties, including the election of national legislators and presidential electors. While there are important informal links between national and state parties, as we saw earlier, we can hardly characterize state parties as branch offices of the national party organization.

Whereas the dominant European tradition is central-party control of constituency-party units, party organizations in the United States function simultaneously on different levels of government, involving different constituencies, needs, and policy problems. The locally based components of the nominal national party are independent of local units elsewhere and of the national party leadership. The de facto relation between state parties and national party is considerably less federal than that between state governments and the national government. Coalition and bargaining, not hierarchy and command, best describe intraparty relationships. Generalizations on the subject are quite tentative, because the relationships that obtain tend to be personal and discontinuous, and to vary by time, circumstance, changing leadership, and the nature of competing power centers.

The national party organization is most developed and unified in presidential-election years, when it capitalizes on the impact of the presidential contest on state-local races. Even then, however, the national party constitutes more a working alliance of local party leaders than an army with a clear chain of command from the center to the field forces. The national party organization's primary focus on the nomination, campaign, and election of a president underscores the sporadic and discontinuous character of its efforts, and its sharing of power with local parties suggests the limits of its authority. By contrast, state and local party organizations, with more frequent elections and their own bases of power, are more continuously active and permit no sharing of control over their own activities.

The operations of the national committee, ostensibly the capstone of the national party organization, index these power limits. The national committee is a representative rather than a power-exercising body; its members are selected by the underlying power bases in each state, and each state is equally represented. A committee meeting is thus a gathering of independent authorities, not of staff subordinates. The committee's powers, derived from the national convention, can be exercised only to the extent encouraged by the national chairman. (The chairman of the party in the White House is invariably the president's man, while the out-party chairman is usually the titular leader's choice or, in conflict situations, an interfactional mediator.) Although the committee does manage the convention, and individual members are important in fund-raising, political intelligence, liaison, organization, and patronage, clearly the national committee is not a party-governing body. It does not control state parties, set national policy lines, nor run the national party between conventions. It is not comparable in presidential nominations to state party organizations in gubernatorial nominations. Except in the case of an incumbent president seeking renomination, the national committee does not agree in advance on any "organizational slate" to be presented to the convention; rather it is deliberately isolated from choosing a presidential nominee. Thus the national committee attempts to service some of the party's needs, but it eschews such dimensions of party governance as setting policy programs, designating favored presidential and vice-presidential nominees, and imposing disciplinary sanctions upon uncooperative or hostile state parties.

The structure of the national party is most truncated in the absence of a presidential contest. At midterm elections the influence of the collective congressional wing of the party is normally higher and congressional candidates are freer to determine their campaigns in personal and idiosyncratic ways. Since the incumbent president enhances his party's legislative unity and public image, the decentralizing forces affect the out-party more, impairing its ability to compete effectively in the legislature. How to locate and sustain authoritative leadership for the out-party, whether it controls one, both, or neither chamber of the Congress, remains a serious problem affecting both the party and the larger political system.

It is a vexing problem because the United States has no counterpart to the recognized status of the British Leader of the Opposition. The defeated presidential candidate or some other party personage could be assigned leadership position by statute, but that would scarcely guarantee him acceptability or power. Some reformers have suggested that the out-party designate its recognized leader by a special convention held midway between presidential elections. But serious presidential aspirants would be loath to bid openly for the nomination so far in advance of the presidential election; nor would a midterm convention be likely to work out a unified policy position. Divorced from the designation of a presidential candidate, any out-party's attempt to hammer out a common issue stance almost surely would promote dissension rather than unity.

Establishing collective leadership for the out-party is yet another possibility, formalized in the Democratic Advisory Council from 1956-1960. But the experience of that short-lived body demonstrates the inherent limitations of such a device. Many congressmen invited to join the Council declined on the grounds that as elected national legislators they could not be bound by policy determined by a Council composed mostly of persons outside the Congress: governors, state party leaders, and party notables. This objection, derived from the most basic perceptions congressmen have of their own place and role in the political system, appears ineradicable. As a consequence the Council became the voice of the liberal presidential wing of the Democrats, countering the conservatism of a congressional leadership frequently unwilling to oppose President Eisenhower. The Council was a useful weapon for a party faction that controlled neither the White House nor the Congress, but it failed by far to become the authoritative leadership of the out-party.

Decentralization and Disloyalty: The Case of the South

The changing political alignments of the South we discussed in Chapter III spawned conflicts between some Southern state parties and the Democratic national party. These disputes were not inevitable; large-scale partisan shifts of the electorate can occur without altering the relations between the state and the party. But the Southern dissidents insisted, even as they supported third-party or Republican presidential candidates, that they remained Democrats in good standing with the national party. The consequent intraparty controversies provide insight into the nature and limits of the decentralization characteristic of a major party, and hence merit brief recounting here.[1]

Our account may conveniently begin with 1948, although seats involving "loyal" and "potentially disloyal" Southern state delegations had been contested in Democratic national conventions earlier. Mississippi, South Carolina, and Alabama, anticipating the nomination of Truman and the adoption of a strong civil rights plank, sent delegations with highly restricted credentials to the convention in order to retain postconvention discretion as to whom each would support. Non-Southern delegations voted to seat these Southern delegations, but they also warned the Deep South states to moderate their incipient rebellion lest they suffer future retaliation. This slap on the wrist did nothing to stay the Deep South, and when the convention later endorsed a strong civil rights plank, the entire Mississippi and half the Alabama delegation dramatically walked off the floor and returned home.

Fueled by the resentments of the Deep South, the States' Rights (or Dixiecrat) third-party movement emerged in 1948. Actually, its preparations were evident well in advance of the national convention: the central strategy of the dissidents was to gain control of the Democratic party in as many Southern states as possible. The Dixiecrats could then not only instruct the state delegation to the national convention, but also determine which presidential electors were on the state ballot, and under what party's designation. In four Deep South states, Mississippi, South Carolina, Louisiana, and Alabama, they succeeded in placing their presidential candidates on the ballot under the emblem of the state Democratic party. The Truman-Barkley ticket also appeared on the ballot in three of these states; Alabama was the only state in the nation omitting the national Democratic ticket. In Florida, neither the Dixiecrat nor Democratic nominees were assigned the state party emblem. In the remaining six Southern states the national Democratic ticket was granted the state party label, and the Dixiecrats had to place an independent or third-party slate on the ballot.

The election results mirrored the Dixiecrats' earlier success or failure in capturing state Democratic parties and in arranging the ballot form to their advantage. Mississippi, South Carolina, Louisiana, and Alabama supplied all the Dixiecrat's electoral votes and over half of its

---

[1] For a fuller account and analysis, see my "The Unsolid South," *op. cit.*; also Abraham Holtzman, *The Loyalty Pledge Controversy in the Democratic Party* (New York: McGraw-Hill Book Company, Eagleton Institute Cases in Practical Politics, No. 21, 1960).

Southern popular vote. The Dixiecrats captured the state party emblem in those Deep South states because of their greater dissidence, but the expropriation of the party label also exerted an independent influence on behalf of the bolters. It strengthened both the legitimacy and popular appeal of their defection, and it procured the support of thousands of voters who habitually backed the Democratic ticket.

The Dixiecrat revolt was a failure: in the extent of its regional backing and in its intent to defeat Truman. But it demonstrated the capacity of the heartland South to defect, not merely to threaten defection. By the 1952 convention it was apparent that defection would recur, though in the form of presidential Republicanism—Republicrats —rather than in continued third-party activity. Hence it fell to the 1952 convention to resolve the thorny intraparty problems raised by the past actions of Southern Dixiecrats and the anticipated actions of Southern Republicrats. These problems centered on the relations between the state party, particularly its delegation to the national convention and its control of presidential electors, and the national party, in the authority of the national convention over state parties and the obligations of a participant state delegation to the convention's nominees.

From the perspective of Southern dissidents, the obligations a state party assumed through its participation in a national convention had to be minimized, if their defection was to succeed. They would be greatly handicapped if convention participation required a state party to place the national ticket on the state ballot under its label and to refrain from openly opposing that ticket in the election. Defection would be stripped of its glamour and made to appear as desertion, and the many votes automatically cast under the state party emblem would work against the dissidents. Nor would it be more effective to refuse to send a delegation to the national convention. This strategy would also stigmatize revolt as desertion, reduce Southern influence within the convention, and invite the national party to create a "loyalist" faction within each rebellious state.

Southern defectors thus advanced a states' rights doctrine of intraparty relations which reserved to themselves the utmost freedom of action within the party without commensurate obligations. They assigned the national party the status of a confederate body in which the constituent units, the state parties, retained nearly autonomous power. Under state laws, it was urged, the state party organs and legislature had exclusive authority to determine the presidential candidates on the ballot and the label. The state delegation could not permit itself to be bound on those matters by the national convention. Acting on these claims, the dissidents sent delegations to the national convention in 1952, expecting on the one hand that they would be seated and participate as fully as any other delegation, and on the other hand reserving the right to confer the state Democratic label and support on someone other than the nominee selected by that national convention.

Though this Southern posture assaulted the very integrity of the national party, practical solutions were not easy. As a representative body, the national convention was of course the final judge of the qualifications of its own members, and a convention majority could impose all sorts of requirements as part of those qualifications. But a presidential victory is seldom gained by ejecting from the convention a sizable number of state party delegations. Moreover, rejection by the convention would buttress the emotional theme of Southern recalcitrants that the Democratic party had deserted the South, and not vice versa. In short, the political consequences of any proposed settlement was never overlooked by most delegates or the contestants for the presidential nomination.

We may skip the detailed maneuverings in this controversy and confine our attention to the 1952 convention and election outcomes. A misnamed loyalty pledge was imposed on all delegates, but it was so ambiguous that Southern dissidents construed it as requiring only that the national ticket appear on the state ballot. Even so, several Southern state delegations refused to accede, yet were ultimately seated by convention vote because Stevenson's backers felt it necessary to resist the efforts of the Harriman-Kefauver forces to oust Southern intransigents. In the ensuing election several Democratic governors, including those of Louisiana, Texas, and South Carolina, led movements for presidential Republicanism. Eisenhower carried four rim-South states in his sweeping national victory. Under the spur of defeat, which provides obvious incentives to reduce internal disunity, the national Democratic party set about to settle the party loyalty issue in ways that would bind up the wounds.

The adoption of three new Democratic party rules by the national committee in 1955 and by the convention in 1956 marked the formal end of the dispute. These rules were the product of an advisory committee that represented the power centers in the state parties, the congressional leadership, and the less extremist partisans on both sides of the 1952 loyalty conflict. The advisory committee, in turn, was the idea of the national chairman, supported by Stevenson as titular leader and officially endorsed by the national committee. Since the convention had not authorized anyone to settle the loyalty controversy, these actions suggest that the usual depiction of the limited authority of the national chairman and committee may be overdrawn.

The first new rule imposed a moral obligation on every state Democratic party sending a delegation to the convention to work to place the convention's nominees on the state ballot "under the Democratic label and designation." The second new rule expressed a good-faith assumption that participating delegates would support the decisions and nominees of the convention. Formal assurances of loyalty could be asked, however, of contested delegations or of delegates challenged because of their past record or their anticipated defection. The third new rule imposed upon members of the national committee the duty "to declare affirmatively for the nominees of the convention." A member's failure to do so was sufficient cause for the committee to declare his seat vacant, after notice and hearing. Finally, the committee member was held to be essentially an appointee of the national convention to the national committee, and not primarily an agent of the state party organization. Hence only the national committee could oust a member before completion of his four-year term of office, and then only for cause.

It would be easy to read these new rules as an affirmation of the decentralized nature of American major parties. As the first rule revealed, since there was no way the convention could legally bind a state party to place the national ticket on the ballot and under its label, the national party depended on the cooperation of its state party affiliates to accomplish those modest objectives. Further, the second rule deliberately refused the requests of loyalist Southerners for the imposition of something like a test oath, and chose instead to rely initially on assumptions of good faith on the part of delegates. Yet rather than dwell on the obvious fact that the national party is considerably less than a centralized governing organization, we should stress that the new rules involve state parties and delegations in commitments which make of the national party something more than just a confederation. Additionally, the status in the national party of a member of the national committee appears to be firmly stated. The critical uncertainty, which requires us to suspend judgment on the impact of the rules, is whether the political capacity to enforce the new obligations exists.

Before the 1960 Democratic convention national chairman Paul Butler and some Northern liberals directed much tough talk to the Deep South on the possibility of challenging their delegates or of forming and accrediting rival delegations unless the South abandoned plans for defection. Though other factors doubtless were more influential, the Deep South's intent to rebel (by running unpledged electors) did wane sharply before convention time. Again in 1964 the convention acknowledged the moral claim of a Mississippi interracial "Freedom Party" delegation, which had no legal standing, and warned the Deep South that delegations selected by procedures that excluded the Negro electorate would be subject to challenge and rejection in subsequent conventions.

These changes doubtless should be interpreted as products of intraparty dissension on the race issue rather than as deliberate steps in the direction of greater national party centralization. But to put the matter that way is to miss the essential point. If there are centralizing tendencies, they derive less from an abstract appreciation of the virtues of centralization than from the increasing indisposition of a party majority to permit an intransigent minority to have its way on a high-priority issue. The push to centralization, no less than the rigid embrace of states' rights, takes on political meaning and force only as it connects with ongoing interests and needs. The same observation applies, as we shall see, in our assessment later in this chapter of centralizing trends in the role of party in the Congress.

Policy Similarity and Policy Ambiguity

At campaign time, the orators of the major parties profess to see momentous policy alternatives between Democrats and Republicans, while minor-party leaders insist that no policy gulf exists between the major parties. Neither view is fully accurate, but the latter is often closer to reality. Thus a common characterization of American major parties is that they are indifferent to policy and frequently indistinguishable in their policy orientations.

Why do American parties shy away from an elaborated ideology, and prefer instead limited policy commitments that are often ambiguous, usually moderate and middle-of-the-road, and frequently similar to the positions of the other party? One essential part of the explanation lies in the power goals of serious parties: their purpose is to win control of government, which must be done through the construction of electoral majorities. And even though party militants and leaders may personally hold to a set of internally consistent issue positions, quite different from those held by their opposition counterparts, election outcomes hinge largely on the response of the mass citizenry. Hence the other major part of the explanation emerges from the setting within which power-oriented parties must operate. Oversimplified, the parties exhibit an ideological bent only to the extent that the broad electorate requires them to do so. The American electorate, in turn, is characterized by a low level of political involvement and by a thinly developed sense of class consciousness, characteristics that produce little pressure on the parties to become ideological or doctrinaire.

The pluralism of social interests, combined with a party's need for wide geographic support, coerces both major parties into adopting similar, moderate policies. The usual party strategy is to try to mobilize a significant degree of support from many interests, rather than to gamble on overwhelming majority support from a few interests. Thus both parties appeal broadly to voters as "citizens," and then make supplemental appeals to the widest possible range of special-interest groups. Since their purpose is to induce support and not to arouse hostility, the appeals are usually couched in equivocal and ambiguous terms, which encourages each citizen to interpret them as he wishes.

This similar generality of appeals from both major parties, in a circularly reinforcing fashion, persuades members of the same income, occupational, religious, ethnic, or regional group to divide in their support of a party. Hence each party attracts something like the same cross-section of the population, rather than exclusive segments. The similarly diverse composition of interests of the major parties further stimulates each to tailor its appeals in like manner. When a special effort to attract the uncommitted middle must be made, as often happens, the pressures on the party to moderate its policies become overwhelming.

Cynics may infer that the parties have no principles at all, and the only distinction between them is that one is in power and the other is not. That inference is wrong. The parties do have principles, but in response to external conditions they tend to be similar rather than sharply different. This interpretation affirms the role of the major parties in promoting social consensus, in reinforcing the predominant values in constitutional democracy, individual rights, and the economy, and in determining the subject matter of issues relevant to politics. The very existence of ideological third parties and their standard complaint of being "frozen out" of the political dialogue testify, after all, to the major parties' possession of some set of principles.

We may also tend to exaggerate the rapidity and ease with which major parties can alter their policy views. Historically, the nondoctrinaire nature of the parties has facilitated profound shifts, in response to changing circumstances or to electoral necessities, in what passes for party doctrine. Defenders of the party system mark this pattern a healthy sign of flexibility, while critics interpret it as the disease of opportunism. Be that as it may, a party must maintain some policy continuity at least from one election to the next in order to reinforce its followers and to demonstrate its integrity.

The role of party in promoting critical shifts in government policy is also understated in the usual description. If one's perspective sets up as the primary datum the proportion of national elections characterized by important issue differences between the parties, the standard view of party indifference to policy is supported. But if the emphasis is on the critical importance of a handful of elections that realigned electoral loyalties and government policies for many decades, and upon the facilitative role of parties in those changes, then the verdict on the relation of party to policy is quite different. (Recall the comments in Chapter I on the possible inappropriateness of popular expectations of the regularity and intensity of party competition in two-party situations. Might not our expectations of the impact of party on policy be similarly excessive?)

As a final item of correction, the diversity of interests embraced by each major party is not as common and overlapping as the customary portrait implies. Both parties draw support from virtually all groups, and each party thus contains strange bedfellows, such as Negroes and white segregationists within the Democratic party. But the parties do not draw equivalent support from all groups, and consequently their interest composition is skewed differently. Since the New Deal, the national Democrats have had a special appeal to urban, union labor, lower class, and newer ethnic groups, and the Republicans to rural-suburban, business, middle class, and old-stock groups. Reflecting these interest mixes, the Democrats have been broadly identified with innovation, reform, and spending, whereas the Republicans have leaned to the status quo and to balanced budgets and savings. These tendencies, of course, are not shared uniformly by the supporters of each party, but they index interparty differences that are recognized impressionistically and account for the different images of the parties held by the citizenry. Sample survey research has demonstrated repeatedly that various demographic groupings of the population favor one party more than the other, and that most respondents continue to perceive the policy complexion of the major parties in terms molded by the events of the Great Depression of the 1930's.

Party and the Congress

The decentralization and localism of American national parties are nowhere better illustrated than in nominations to national legislative offices. A core power of any centralized party organization is approval or rejection of party candidacies for the national legislature. American national party organizations have no right of control, nor even of collaboration, and any informal influence they may care to muster is limited in scope and often circumspect in application.

The tradition of local autonomy in Senate and House nominations has fattened on the failure of the two large efforts by national party leadership in this century to purge party ranks in the Congress. In 1910 conservative Republicans led by President Taft and Senator Aldrich sought unsuccessfully to deny renomination to several western Progressive Republicans. In 1938 President Roosevelt had some success (and some failures) in striving to unseat several policy opponents within the party, mostly from the South, but at the high cost of intensifying Southern resistance to his programs within the Congress. These experiences have affirmed the norm of national nonintervention generally, particularly if an incumbent legislator is seeking renomination. The national leadership at times has a bit more opportunity, providing the state party is amenable, to promote a particular candidacy when the opposition candidate is the incumbent.

But it does not invariably follow that because national party influence is confined the state or district party organization takes over legislative nominations. National legislators tend to be poorly integrated into the state party structure, and frequently develop personal organizations that assure easy renomination, especially after some years of incumbency. This pattern is characteristic of U. S. Representatives, since House districts are seldom important units of state party organization. The direct primary, if it is not under the control of a handful of party leaders, is also useful to an incumbent legislator's ability to develop and capitalize on a personal organization. This diffusion of power means that even if the national party leadership wanted to intervene, it could not find a control point to influence or negotiate with.

The decentralization of legislative nominations, and the inflation of localism and personalism, deprives the national party of perhaps the most critical mechanism of imposing party discipline. The quality of candidates, no less than their policy directions, is left to local fate and control. Little wonder that a group's policy protest is often influential within the predominant local party, without the group having to shift party allegiances; or that each party's set of national legislators encompasses in the aggregate a wide range of issue positions.

Parochial factors play a lesser role in electing national legislators than in nominating them. Since the established view emphasizes the idiosyncratic quality of many congressional elections, some compensating stress in the other direction might be warranted. We have discussed earlier (in Chapters II and III) aspects of the interlocking preferences of the electorate in presidential and congressional races, which indicate the linking of the two in the minds of the voters. Election outcomes in competitive districts (or "marginal districts") are most affected by this link, which presumably sensitizes legislators from such districts to their stake in the overall record of their party and of the president. The relaxation of the linkage at midterm elections gives freer play to localistic and individualistic factors, but the midterm verdict is only incompletely divorced from electoral judgments of party and president. Here again the marginal-district legislators are most vulnerable to adverse voter reaction, and hence they have the greatest incentive to promote party performance within the chamber that appeals to the voters. Even legislators of the president's party from less competitive districts may feel obliged to support him because the president has usually carried their legislative districts. By the same reasoning, safe-district legislators have less need to cooperate with the party majority, and because the predominance of a single interest often underlies one-partyism, they experience compelling constituency pressure to defect on matters affecting that interest.

On the role of party politics in the operations of the Congress, factors that promote or disrupt party influence interact uneasily, providing evidence for both the established view and some revision of it. Experience suggests that a legislative body, acting by itself and through its own resources, cannot produce coordinated and disciplined legislative parties, nor can it provide the unity, leadership, and policy initiative required in a prolonged Cold War period. Legislative dependency upon the executive in these matters is apparently a necessity, expressed in the British scheme by the role of the Cabinet and in the American by the legislative leadership role of the president. While the latter is a development that is altering the traditional relations between executive and legislative branches, it has not reached executive dominance, and still is characterized more by collaboration and influence than by command and control. As an independent branch of the government, the Congress retains an institutional interest in at least partial and occasional resistance to presidential leadership, notwithstanding its dependence on it.

In form, party is pervasive in the structure and functioning of the Congress. To take one example, the majority party within the chamber controls the organizational posts of power: all committee chairmanships, a majority of the membership of each committee, the Speakership of the House, and the like. But in the committees—whose work is the principal determinant of legislative outcomes—the assignment of members and chairmen by the rule of seniority often works against party and presidential influence. This rule favors, within each party, legislators and interests from districts which tend to return the same legislators election after election, that is, one-party districts, usually rural, frequently characterized by a pronounced single interest, social stability, and conservatism. The seniority leaders are not a cross-section of the legislative party; and they are least dependent upon the record of the party and the president for their own re-election chances. This fractionation of structural authority, combined with the complexities of legislative procedure that benefit status quo interests seeking to delay or obstruct, exemplifies and accentuates the diffusion of power broadly associated with American government. When we add the diverse constituencies and interests represented within each party's legislative camp, the stage is set for deviations from party voting, a pattern emphasized by many commentators in their depiction of the relation of party to legislature.

Although clearly party lines are less than firm in the Congress, it would be seriously wrong to adjudge party only marginally relevant to legislative behavior. For one thing, the median policy position of Democratic legislators does differ from the Republican legislators' and in a direction consistent with the popular image of the parties. For another, the best single predictor of legislative alignments is the party label of the legislators. A focus on the conspicuous party deviance of Demo-

cratic Senator Harry Byrd of Virginia or of Republican Senator Jacob
Javits of New York properly attests to voting across party lines, but we
should not forget that the numerical norm remains party constancy.
Virtually all the legislators of a party vote far more frequently with
their party than against it, and defections are not undertaken lightly or
routinely. The president's party is likely to be more unified than the
out-party, reflecting the policy impetus supplied by the president and
his continuous collaboration with the elective legislative party leaders.
Indeed, the greater disunity and policy inertia of the legislative out-
party, which gravely handicaps its functioning as an "alternative government," is a defect in the party system that merits more attention
than the absence of tight party lines on many roll-call votes.

As we implied earlier, few effective sanctions are readily available
to the party leadership by which they can force policy unity on a
legislative party inclined otherwise. In fact, policy deviance because of
the needs of the constituency is acceptable legislative behavior and
does not merit retaliation. The difficulties of imposing sanctions can
best be illustrated in a matter widely viewed as a party transgression—
namely, a legislator's open support for another party's presidential candidate. Of the few Southern congressmen who stumped for the Dixiecrats in 1948 and of the many who remained neutral, none was denied
his regular committee assignment, including chairmanships. Nor was
Democratic Representative Adam Clayton Powell punished by the
legislative party for his open support of Eisenhower in 1956. Similarly,
in 1960, the slimness of Kennedy's election victory and working majority in the Congress militated against punitive action against Southern
Democrats who had supported Nixon or "free electors." In 1964, in the
context of lopsided Democratic majorities in both chambers, two Deep
South congressmen who had supported Goldwater were denied their
committee positions by the Democratic caucus, and one subsequently
chose to become a Republican. This record underscores both the political context within which sanctions must be considered, and how infrequently the legislative party is willing or able to punish actions that
violate even the loose American standards of party regularity.

Since party retaliation for election disloyalty remains possible,
whereas policy deviance is virtually immune from party punishment,
most Southern congressmen disenchanted with the national Democrats
have opted for the latter. For such legislators, advocating Democratic
party regularity in elections paradoxically becomes the most persistent
Southern technique of de facto party defection. Former Governor

Cameron Morrison, a North Carolina leader, advised his state delegation in the 1952 Democratic convention how they should react to the "party loyalty" pledge:

> We've been Democrats too long to let any hotheads drive us out of the party. . . . We are probably going to get a terrible platform plank on civil rights. But we've had planks we didn't like before, and our representatives and senators have been able to beat them off in Congress. . . . After all, so long as we can hold powerful places in the Congress, the President can recommend all he wants to, but he still can't get his bills through if our fellows won't help him.

Such a calculating exploitation of party raises starkly the contrast between "nominal" and "real" party membership, which agitates the critics of the present party system, as we will see in the next chapter. Yet in this, as in so many other aspects of intraparty relationships, centralizing changes are less likely to come from logical arguments than from interfactional conflict within the party, such as that between South and non-South or between liberals and conservatives. In recent sessions of the Senate liberals have repeatedly sought to alter the rules to make it easier to impose curbs on the filibuster, and in the House in early 1965 the Speaker was given authority to compel the Rules Committee, three weeks after its receipt of a bill, to discharge it for floor consideration.

Given the national party's restricted ability to apply sanctions, achieving greater cohesion within the legislative party may well depend on whether the districts won by the party are less diverse in their composition than at present and, hence, are more homogeneous in policy outlook. Should this trend develop, and some of the critics of party urge that it will, the analyst would find it difficult to disentangle the constituency from the party aspects of the more highly unified legislative party. That distinction, however, might become moot for all except purists, since presumably a unified party, whatever the source of its unity, would behave in more centralized patterns than currently. This line of argument is admittedly speculation and not prediction, but at least it reminds us that the constituency factor, commonly treated as the rival to the party influence factor, often undergirds party influence and accounts for high as well as low levels of party unity.

Party and the Electorate

One criterion facilitating an effective contrast between one- and two-party systems, it will be recalled from Chapter II, was the extent to which each system meaningfully structured election choice for voters. The utility of party in this and related functions merits amplification here, some details of which may be surprising because they run counter to prevailing attitudes linking party and citizenry. These attitudes include, on the one hand, a derogation of partisanship and partisan commitment (a "blind partisan," a "party liner," etc.), and on the other, approval of political independency ("I vote for the best man regardless of party," the Burkean concept of the legislator, etc.). Given these attitudes, the findings on the importance of party to voter motivation are striking, and they perhaps suggest, as the critics of our party system argue, that Americans might be receptive to more centralized parties.

Careful sample survey analysis of the motivations of the mass electorate in recent presidential elections has demonstrated the central relevance of party attachment to voter behavior.[2] The concept of "party identification," treated in terms of the individual's own perceptions, refers to the intensity of his psychological identification with a particular party, as determined by his responses to structured questions put to him by the interviewer. By this measure, for the period of contemporary politics about 33 percent locate themselves as Strong Democrats or Republicans, about 40 percent as Weak Democrats or Republicans, and about 12 percent as Independent Democrats or Republicans; the remaining 15 percent divide about equally between Independents and those deemed to be apolitical. In terms of self-perception, then, the majority of American adults is attached to a major party, and psychological independence of party is characteristic of few. The Democrats have about a three-to-two edge in party identification distributions in all three categories. Most people take on their party identification, Democratic or Republican, during their adolescence as part of a larger process of political socialization. The family, therefore, is the instrument that maintains party attachment from one generation to the next. Over the individual's own life cycle party identification typically

---

[2] This section refers to and draws upon the major published works on voting behavior of the Survey Research Center of the University of Michigan, especially Angus Campbell *et al.*, *The American Voter* (New York: John Wiley & Sons, 1960).

is durable, and increases in intensity the longer the individual is attached to the same party.

The party identification factor is important because it structures political attitudes and behavior in persistent and predictable ways. An individual's sense of attachment to party functions as a perceptual screen which sharply confines the amount and kind of external political stimuli he is willing to receive, and which evaluates partisanly what he does take in. By such selective perception and other mechanisms associated with the individual's need for consistency, party identification becomes self-reinforcing, and the voter insulates himself from external happenings that might contradict, and therefore threaten to change, his party ties.

Most citizens are only slightly aware of the issue dimension of politics, and they are relatively insensitive to interparty policy differences that may emerge in a presidential campaign. (Sports, not politics, appears to be the true year-round avocation of Americans.) Barring the sudden upthrust of a dramatic issue or candidacy, most people vote largely as an expression of their enduring party tie. For those who are more involved with issues, the predominant pattern is a rough congruence between party attachment and issue position, with each reinforcing the other but with the main line of causation for most running from party tie to issue preference.

Presidential election outcomes need not be, though many are, mere ratifications of the underlying party identifications of the electorate. The correlation of party identification with actual vote behavior, while invariably positive in the expected direction, varies in strength from election to election because of idiosyncratic campaign elements: an appealing issue, or a candidate at odds with the party predisposition of many voters. We would expect a higher proportion of self-designated Strong Republicans than Strong Democrats to vote Republican in each election, but we would also expect the percent within each partisan camp actually voting for their party's candidate to vary from one election to the next. This variability explains, in the current period of a Democratic edge in party identification, why Republicans can win (1952 and 1956) and why a Democratic victory can be oversize (1964). Whether such voter shifts signify a transient straying or a more enduring realignment of electoral attachments is obviously an object of close investigation by practical politicians and professional analysts alike.

Helpful inferences emerge from even so abbreviated an account of party and the electorate. For example, the key characteristics of the party identification factor neatly complement the findings we discussed in Chapter I: of the pattern of alternating periods of one-party control in presidential politics; and of the pronounced tendency of the major parties to compete within a persistent 60-40 percent division of the two-party popular vote. Campaign strategists find useful the inference that a majority party, in determining how best to apply its limited resources, must never fail to emphasize the activation and reinforcement of its own partisans. The minority party could profit by the same admonition, but it also somehow has to mute the partisanship of its appeals in order to attract the uncommitted, and perhaps make some inroads on the opposition ranks as well. Yet another inference is that major and massive voter realignments are unlikely in the absence of a crisis of Civil War or Great Depression magnitude.

The real world of party identifiers contrasts starkly with the picture of the "democratic citizen" so pervasive in our civics texts and political rhetoric. It is partisans, not independents, who are most intensely interested and involved in politics. In noncrisis times partisan ties are neither fluid nor easily susceptible to change, and these enduring attachments shape the receipt of political information and the perception of political issues and events far more than campaign communications and events shape party choice. It is a nice question, disputatious to political scientists and philosophers alike, whether our concept of what constitutes good citizenship should be altered in the light of these and allied empirical findings on voter behavior, or whether we should strengthen efforts to reform behavior in line with the retained norms. Whatever the answer, the findings demonstrate that the average voter depends heavily upon party and party system to simplify, impose order on, and give meaning to his political world.

Chapter V

CRITICISM, DEFENSE, AND TRENDS

For many years commentators have disputed the adequacy of the American party system, especially as discussed in the preceding chapter, its decentralized, undisciplined, and nonprogrammatic character. Foreign observers, disturbed by the pronounced American departure from European party experience, often render negative verdicts. And many American analysts, usually of a liberal outlook, also have found the party system seriously wanting. The volume, tone, and direction of the dispute have been affected, of course, by changing external events. During the late 1930's the writing reflected the economic depression and the threat of major war, and stridently attacked the diffusion of power of American institutional arrangements and party practices as fatally impairing the capacities of government. After America's victory in the Second World War and its emergence as the greatest non-Communist power, the post-1945 commentaries tended to be more moderate and sanguine in evaluating American political processes. The variability during the past several decades in the saliency and intensity of the controversy should not obscure the fact that it continues to occupy the attention of professional analysts and practicing politicians. Few studies of parties or congressional sessions slight the problem of reforming, revitalizing, or otherwise changing our party system. And few students taking college courses that deal with American parties fail to muse on significantly altering the party system.

By closely reviewing the disputed judgments of our party system, we are at the same time appraising the strengths and weaknesses of that system. And since much of the evaluation rests on the fit of the party sytem to the larger political process, our analysis also ranges broadly. We here take the CPP *Report* as representative of the adverse position on American parties—often termed the "party government" doctrine.[1] Following our dissection of this *Report*, we close by discussing appropriate directions of reform that derive from, and can be sustained by, current political trends.

The British Model

"The standards for judging party government in the United States have been based most persistently upon norms derived from studying the Mother of Parliaments."[2] Some critics believe that the longevity and maturity of the British party system make it a model toward which other two-party systems must naturally evolve. Not even the evident uniqueness of the British scheme dissuades these commentators from applying such a faulty determinism. Other critics look to British parties not as the "truest" system, but simply as superior to the American counterpart. They feel the British system is both rational and simpli-

---

[1] Committee on Political Parties of the American Political Science Association, *Toward a More Responsible Two-Party System*, Supplement to *American Political Science Review*, 44 (September 1950). The CPP was composed of sixteen professional political scientists, nearly all specialists on political parties, and was chaired by Professor E. E. Schattschneider. The *Report*, while the subject of ongoing debate within the profession, is generally viewed as the most systematic statement of the "party government" position.

[2] Pendleton Herring, *The Politics of Democracy* (New York: Rinehart & Company, 1940), p. 101.

fied, providing "party government" in the full sense of the terms "party" and "government."

Exponents of this view would perhaps subscribe to the following description of British politics. By means of a single election at which voters choose only between parliamentary party candidates, who stand for policies consistent with fellow party candidates and different from the opposition party, a majority party is automatically returned. That majority party becomes *the* Government through Cabinet control, based on party, of the legislative party in Commons. The bureaucracy functions to serve the Government, while the minority party assumes the role of authoritative critic of the Government, and constitutes the alternate government in the event of electoral defeat of the in-party. The governing party bears full responsibility for the product of politics, a fair burden because it possesses full authority. Finally, through various devices of intraparty democracy, both major parties manage to combine centralized discipline with meaningful party membership.

Clearly, such a view of the British party system is idealized. Interparty policy differences and intraparty democracy are less extensive than supposed, and the price of Cabinet omnipotence is the sharp constriction of the role of the legislator. And it is easy to dismiss the relevance of the British experience for American parties precisely because it is both British and parliamentarian. But little would be learned by treating these views in such straw-man terms, and much would be gained by interpreting them in their strongest form, and then engaging in substantive evaluation. When so interpreted, they raise important questions, such as the relationships between party systems and the total complex of government institutions, social structure, and prevailing community beliefs.

Few critics since the 1930's, after all, have seriously urged Americans to adopt the parliamentary form. The moderate reform goals stress more integrated executive-legislative relations or greater party responsibility, or both. What is urged, in short, is a strengthening of political control over the Congress and the bureaucracy by the president, acting through the medium of party. A de facto concentration of political power would thus be substituted for the current dispersion of power, perhaps without extensive formal alteration of existing institutions. So restated, the critics' position appears more practicable and "American," and points the way to the major and often inarticulated premises underlying the willingness to use British experience as the norm. The conflicting evaluation of the American party system is rooted in a profound disparity in the conception of democracy, particularly in the relation of majority rule to democracy. Ultimately one's preferences as to what constitutes good government may well determine the position one takes in the controversy on party.

The Party Government Argument

The CPP capsules its central thesis as follows:

Historical and other factors have caused the American two-party system to operate as two loose associations of state and local organizations, with very little national machinery and very little national cohesion. As a result, either major party, when in power, is ill-equipped to organize its members in the legislative and the executive branches into a government held together and guided by the party program. Party responsibility at the polls thus tends to vanish. This is a very serious matter, for it affects the very heartbeat of American democracy. It also poses grave problems of domestic and foreign policy in an era when it is no longer safe for the nation to deal piecemeal with issues that can be disposed of only on the basis of coherent programs.[3]

The critics urge that of the political mechanisms available only the party system can consistently provide national and rational programs which the electorate can pass on and which are then translated into public law and policy. The party system is thus a central determinant of the character of the government system, capable of bringing about the greater rationalization of political institutions demanded of modern American government. But given the nature of the current party system, it would first have to be thoroughly revamped.

Briefly, the CPP's objective in altering the party system is better integrated and more responsible parties. "Better integrated" means a more conscious policy role for party, greater resistance to localistic and interest-group demands, and a greater commitment to party loyalty and discipline. "More responsible" involves both external responsibility to the voters at elections and internal responsibility (intraparty democracy) to the party rank-and-file. The goal is thus a congruence of electing, representing, and governing functions within the new context of a policy-oriented party system. By restructuring political choice meaningfully for voters and by unified control of government institu-

---

[3] CPP Report, p. v.

tions, parties would operate more or less under mandates to convert electoral verdicts into legislation. The out-party, now also disciplined and committed to coherent policy programs, would function as a true alternative government.

Before this chapter concludes, we shall flesh out these bare bones of the CPP's advocacy, and we shall have examined the important aspects of this reform argument. At this early stage, it is convenient to treat three problems raised by the CPP's position: interparty policy differences, intraparty democracy, and the relation of party leaders to elective leaders.

Critics agree on several aspects of policy-oriented parties. They urge parties to stand unambiguously for the policies they profess to hold, and to exercise more initiative in shaping public awareness of these issues. Some critics stress issue-concerned parties and others dwell on disciplined parties but the practical difference is small, because programmatic parties necessitate inner discipline, and disciplined parties are expected to pursue policy goals. Most critics probably would want parties to have a wide range of issue commitments, but they would not insist on a full-blown ideology. The critics divide more noticeably, though, on how extensive and intense interparty policy differences should become. Their preferences vary all the way from endorsing persistent class conflict to accepting slight modifications of the status quo. On this matter the CPP is clearly closer to the latter position:

> *Needed clarification of party policy* in itself *will not cause the parties to differ more fundamentally or more sharply than they have in the past.* The contrary is much more likely to be the case. The clarification of party policy may be expected to produce a more reasonable discussion of public affairs, more closely related to the political performance of the parties in their actions rather than their words. *Nor is it to be assumed that increasing concern with their programs will cause the parties to erect between themselves an ideological wall.* There is no real ideological division in the American electorate, and hence programs of action presented by responsible parties for the voter's support could hardly be expected to reflect or strive toward such division.[4]

---

[4] *Ibid.,* pp. 20-21. Italics in original.

Assuming that relatively few and modest issue differences divide the parties, the CPP objective is to have those differences expressed clearly and put into practice, rather than obscured.

The CPP's commitment to intraparty democracy, however, seems to run counter to its desire for either moderate policy divergence between the parties or for disciplined parties. Issue-oriented parties sustaining a mass membership and operating by democratic procedures are likely to lean to issue extremism. When the principal basis of attraction to a party is a set of issue positions, the pressures generated by leadership competition and by the need to hold membership loyalties exaggerate the concern for uncompromising issue stands. If, on the other hand, such a party sought to cater to interests more diverse than its dedicated ideologues, intraparty democracy would work against discipline. In a democratically run organization, after all, a focus on issues constitutes a standing invitation to dissension. It is no accident that the disciplined and programmatic European parties of the Left have little truck with the mechanisms of intraparty democracy. The concept of intraparty democracy may thus be rejected because of its lack of fit with the rest of the CPP package, but this does not discredit the overall party government doctrine. Intraparty democracy is not a logically necessary part of that doctrine, and Schattschneider himself, chairman of the CPP, does not subscribe to it. In his own writings, Schattschneider holds to a narrow conception of party membership as confined to party activists, and stresses the contribution of interparty competition rather than intraparty democracy to the effective functioning of party.

Political centralization based on a changed party system raises the prickly question of the relation between leaders of the party organization and elected public officials belonging to that party. Public officials must attempt to serve two dissimilar constituencies, their party membership and the citizenry, and their actions on behalf of the one may at times harm the other. In such circumstances what should be the guidelines for public officials?

One answer defines the problem away by merging the two constituencies into a single identity, that of party members. In a context of intraparty democracy and of mandate-style issue elections, it is argued, the public official should be bound by the party's policies. Their moral force derives from their endorsement by a party majority, an electoral majority, and the public official himself when campaigning. Totalitarian one-party nations typically operate by such a de facto fusion of party and government leaders, with the former controlling the latter as well as the party. European programmatic parties of the non-Communist Left often approach a similar fusion, but the party and policy role of government leaders is far greater.

In the United States the customary answer, except in boss-and-machine situations, is to subordinate the party organization leadership to the government leadership. In view of the importance to the party of contesting elections, office holders and office seekers naturally tend to dominate the party, and often they use the party organization as vehicles of election. The apparatus of the national party in control of the White House, for instance, operates within boundaries and in ways set by the wishes of the president, and it constitutes no base of rival power to him. Within weeks after John F. Kennedy assumed the presidency in 1961 the Democratic Advisory Council was disbanded. Explaining the move, Democratic national chairman John Bailey stressed the inappropriateness of that body once the Democrats had become the in-party—that is, party policy would now be set by the president, and not by any part of the national party machinery.

Legislative parties would prefer, obviously, that party organizations confine themselves to electing rather than policy-setting functions, but in either case they would resent treatment as mere agents of the organizational leadership. Separation of powers accentuates this tendency, and sensitizes members of the Congress to their own distinctive place and needs. The reluctance of legislators to participate in the Democratic Advisory Council, as we noted earlier, represented an institutional and role reaction, not one peculiar to the Democratic factionalism of the time. Members of the legislative party share a sense of separateness, distinctiveness, and self-sufficiency which militates against their control by the national party organization, and which occasionally provokes their resistance to presidential party leadership as well. Given the flabbiness of the national party machinery, the typical intraparty conflict is, therefore, between leaders of the congressional and presidential wings, and not between either or both on the one hand, and on the other the leaders of the external party organization.

The source of initiative for the party programs backed by the legislative party is thus virtually never the national platform as such. And because of the disabilities of contemporary legislatures, only seldom is it the legislative party leadership. In most cases the president and the executive branch supply the policy leadership. Hence perhaps we should understand the CPP's concern to develop policy parties as an effort to enlarge the president's leadership role. If so, we may then ask whether such a development might not be an alternative to, rather than an achievement of, party government. The British system is not, after all, simply a prime-minister system, but a broad cabinet government system based on party. And what of the constricted role of legislators, perhaps justifiable in the setting of cabinet government but not in a separation-of-powers system? The CPP's case is weakened by its handling of these problems of how to relate party to government leaders and presidential to party government.

Party as Independent Influence

We may assume that the CPP did not consider its report a utopian exercise, and that the committee members believed their recommendations for change were practicable. Their suggested reforms, like all reforms, must be rooted in some conceptions of causality within the political system: what factors will bring change and what effects will certain changes have? Identifying those conceptions, especially since they are seldom openly stated in the *Report,* facilitates a deeper appraisal of the party government position.

The most basic assumption of the CPP locates the party system centrally in the functioning of the overall government. It asserts that the party system is capable of fundamentally altering the meaning of elections, the policy component of elections, institutional operations, and the like. And this capability is viewed as unique to party, because party can link citizens to government by representing and coordinating the widest range of interests, and it can centralize control over diverse government centers of policy-making power. From these conceptions of centrality and uniqueness it is only a short step to the position that the party sysem should more or less monopolize these matters.

What will bring about the changes in party? One instructive clue is that the *Report* proposes limited institutional changes, such as reform of the Electoral College, a four-year term for U. S. Representatives, equitable legislative representation, legislative procedures facilitating majority rule, the short ballot, the closed primary, and permanent voter registration. These proposed changes leave intact the most basic institutional forces: the separation of powers and federalism, and the major formal arrangements spawned by them. It follows that the CPP must believe that the essential nature of the party can be altered even though the institutional frame of government remains mostly intact. The conception of causality, in other words, is that the character of American parties is *not* fixed by the formal government structure.

What, then, determines the nature of the party? The CPP's answer is that the party can readily transform itself by its own actions. Whether the party is willing to do so depends on certain internal relationships, which again involve additional conceptions of causality. In the CPP's view, party structure shapes party policy more than the reverse, and effective reform of the party structure must move from the national down to the local level.

The notions of causality underlying the *Report* thus add up to an insistence that the party system is more an independent cause than a dependent effect. This perspective enables the CPP to argue that on the one hand party can be thoroughly revamped within the present institutional context, and on the other that changes in party will bring in their wake basic alterations in the conduct of government and politics. The way to party reform is thus clear—if only the will to reform party exists. As the CPP cautiously puts it:

> Actually the parties have not carefully explored the opportunities they have for more responsible operation under existing constitutional arrangements. It is logical first to find out what can be done under present conditions to invigorate the parties before accepting the conclusion that action has to begin with changing a constitutional system that did not contemplate the growing need for party responsibility when it was set up.[5]

As put more exuberantly by Schattschneider in his own earlier writings:

> Nor are there grounds for excessive pessimism about the possibilities of integrating party government with the constitutional system. The greatest difficulties in the way of the development of party government in the United States have been intellectual, not legal. It is not unreasonable to suppose that once a respectable section of the public understands the issue, ways of promoting party government through the Constitution can be found.[6]

---

[5] *Ibid.,* p. 36.
[6] E. E. Schattschneider, *Party Government* (New York: Rinehart & Company, 1942), pp. 209-210.

We can produce any kind of party system that we have the intelligence and the energy to create.[7]

The central rebuttal to this view asserts, of course, that party is more of a dependent effect and less of an independent cause than the *Report* posits, such as the following blunt statement:

The party system, precisely because it is directed toward the control of government, will closely resemble the government's pattern. If the government is divided federally and functionally, the effort to control it will be similarly dispersed.[8]

A variation of this rebuttal stresses the dependency of party change on the controlling value preferences of the society:

. . . if the Committee really wishes to see genuinely effective *and* democratic government achieved in the United States, it must, however "impractical" it may seem, work for popular acceptance of the *whole* package of majority-rule democracy; it is highly impractical to plead just for a responsible party system which after all is just one part of the total democratic package— and one which logically comes rather late in the argument. . . .

The problem we face is not one of deciding whether the constitutional system or the parties should be changed "first." The point is that the same popular beliefs about government which sustain our present anti-majoritarian constitutional system will continue to sustain (as they have for a very long time) our anti-majoritarian party system. Only when the American people have fully accepted the doctrine of majority-rule democracy can the doctrine of responsible party government expect to receive the popular acclaim which . . . it has so far been denied.[9]

(It is pertinent to remember that the British party system does operate within a commitment to majority-rule democracy.) Hence the rejoinder to the CPP's causal conceptions is that a cohesive, disciplined, and policy-oriented American party system, whether thought of as deriving largely from sanctions or from consensus, is encouraged by

---

[7] E. E. Schattschneider, *The Struggle for Party Government* (College Park, Md.: University of Maryland, 1948), p. 12.

[8] Carl J. Friedrich, *Constitutional Government and Democracy* (Boston: Ginn and Company, rev. ed., 1950), p. 419.

[9] Austin Ranney, "Toward a More Responsible Two-Party System: A Commentary," *American Political Science Review.* 45 (June 1951), p. 499. Italics in original.

neither the ongoing government structure nor the dominant political values. It may well be that the major parties have not adequately exploited the opportunities for greater party unity available in the present structure, but this view is some distance from maintaining that a unified party system is achievable in spite of the present structure.

The prospects for an altered party system are thus more dependent upon contextual and environmental changes than the CPP is prepared to concede. Yet another part of the CPP's argument, next examined, implicitly accepts this corrected view, and hence invites judgment as to its compatability with the CPP position thus far dissected.

External Factors Promoting Party Government

Most reform arguments do not rest content with asserting the need for reform and the merits of their prescriptions, but also attempt to demonstrate feasibility by linking the reforms to ongoing trends. The CPP *Report* is no exception to this tendency, even though it necessarily involves treating the party as a dependent effect of certain external factors. Though this second approach does not jibe with the one just reviewed, it clearly merits evaluation in its own right.

This second approach of the CPP proceeds by analogy. The formal structure of American government has remained reasonably intact through time, whereas effective power has tended to shift from the state and local units to the national government, and from ad hoc, localized interest groups to permanently organized national interest groups. Several inferences are drawn. One is 'hat the trends in the shift of government power constitute a set of external factors that pressure to change the party system in the same direction. It is anomalous for a decentralized party system to hope to cope with centralized Big Government. Another inference is that the shift from sectional to nationalized politics, to a politics dominated by Big Labor, Big Business, and the like, constitutes a set of pressures which *must* move the party system in the same direction. "The measurable shift from sectional to national politics cannot fail to have a corresponding effect on party organization and the locus of power within the parties."[10] The final inference is that, similarly to the shift of government power, the political party can achieve greater de facto centralization without many serious revisions of the formal structure of government.

---

[10] CPP *Report,* p. 33.

There are obvious logical difficulties in indicting contemporary party organization as pre-Civil War in nature, and then arguing that it will or must reflect centralizing tendencies in government power. The implication that party organization is basically a derivative of actual government relationships clashes, of course, with the CPP's causal notions earlier treated. Moreover, if we accept this second view of party as dependent effect, then what explains why the government power balance has responded to nationalizing historical forces and the party power balance has not? Any simple notion of a "culture lag" of party leaders, or of the ultimate inevitability of party change, leaving unspecified the critical factors of the rate of change and timing, begs rather than answers that question.

The value of this second approach of the CPP rests on a careful assessment of the nature and probable consequences of the current "nationalizing forces" to which they refer. These forces include such trends as the diffusion of industry, urbanizaton, and unionization throughout the nation; the increasing scope and saliency of national issues and the concomitant decline of localism and sectionalism; the gradual dissolution of ethnic-religious blocs; the national organization and membership of large-scale interest groups; and the revolution in the mass media of communications.

The broad and eventual effects of these nationalizing forces do push in the direction desired by the proponents of party government. As states and regions diversify the mix of their politically relevant interests, a dilution of pre-existing one-partyism should follow. As an increasing proportion of states becomes more competitive in presidential and state politics, regional dissidence should lessen and centralizing tendencies in the national parties should strengthen. On the local level there is already one obvious sign of a more uniform and truly national electorate: the decline of the old-style political machine and the emergence of reformers whose penetration of the urban party organization is motivated largely by their national and state issue concerns.

Yet these forces are still too recent to give us the extent and rate of homogenization of the national citizenry. Until we know these, the suspicion persists that the CPP may be too optimistic. Just because a rural area is moving in the direction of greater industrialization, its economy will not necessarily converge with that of the rest of the nation. Then, too, the development of a steel plant or of a petro-chemical complex has political implications quite different from those associated with cotton milling or timber processing. Nor does the rest of the nation stand still while underdeveloped domestic areas step up their rate of industrialization. Hence we may reasonably expect that politically significant economic differences among many areas will continue to exist for some time.

Similar caveats apply to the overly simple proposition that a decline in the older forms of sectionalism automatically ushers in a nationalized politics. Issues will remain—race relations, farm policy, regulation of trade unions, and the like—whose impact will not be felt evenly in all areas of the nation. Should these sorts of issues become paramount, something akin to the older sectionalism may persist in response to them. On the other hand, sectional and class reactions to national politics presumably would diminish if foreign policy issues became predominant. These comments are not meant to invite dispute over second-guessing the future, but to suggest that the easy political inferences usually drawn from the nationalizing-forces argument should be considered both premature and uncertain.

The Normative Quarrel

Defenders of the American party system are fond of asserting that whereas they believe the character of a party system must match its larger government context, the advocates of party government do not. That assertion is false. Recall that the *Report* urges that centralizing political forces must move the party system toward greater centralization, and nevertheless that a self-transformed party system will produce congruent changes in the larger political system. In neither case can we tax the CPP position with denying that the degree of fit between party and contextual political system must remain close.

The real disagreement between critics and defenders turns on the former's contention, and the latter's denial, that the party by its own actions can alter its nature and its political environment. The defense position need not quarrel with the view, advanced in both the *Report* and this volume, that because of the scope and depth of its impact the party system must be located nearer to the center than the margins of the political process. But the defense position must and does indict the CPP for abstracting party artificially from its shaping context by exaggerating the party's capacity to revamp itself and its environment. Party, in the defense view, remains more a dependent effect than an independent cause.

The case against the party government doctrine could rest on the preceding grounds alone, and some commentators have done just that. For our purposes, however, pushing the argument further proves fruitful. Whereas our analysis thus far has dealt with the question of whether the CPP's goals *can* be achieved, we now shift to the question of whether those goals *should* be achieved, that is, the normative dimension of the disagreement.

We have tried to show that critics and defenders alike agree that the party system cannot be greatly dissimilar from its setting. So, too, both sides would say that the American party system has been functionally appropriate to the larger political system. By this we do not mean, of course, that every aspect of party structure and operations would be deemed justifiable and beyond criticism, or that specific reform proposals would meet with a uniform reaction. Rather, the evidence is overwhelming that the fundamental characteristics of the party system are more in harmony than in conflict with the dispersion of power pervading the overall system.

Criticism of the party system, therefore, is at bottom criticism of the basic system of which it is a part. And while the former is the ostensible target, the latter is often the real target. Many party government proponents really aim at revising the larger system and merely use the party as the mechanism of change. The primacy of this broader objective explains why the critics impose oversize tasks on the party and exaggerate the independence and plasticity of the party system. The party government doctrine thus poses a basic challenge: is the contextual political system, to which the party system must conform, effective? Reacting to this challenge, those defending the party system often forego a direct defense in favor of justifying the larger system, of which party is but one of many integrated parts. In this manner the normative aspects of the party government quarrel become effectively joined.

The opposed beliefs are too divergent for reconciliation. Critics support Woodrow Wilson's thesis that "the more power is divided, the more irresponsible it becomes"; defenders believe the opposite. Emphasizing the pluralism of interests in the nation, defenders infer the primacy of the quest for greater unity and consensus, not greater social division and conflict, and for protection of individual rights, not the strengthening of the power of the majority. Critics stress policy, policy consistency, and policy choice; defenders assert the need for compromise and assign no priority to a focus on issues. What one side sees as promoting a desirable clarification of issue choice for the electorate the other side interprets as fostering party rigidity and sectional or class cleavage. The composition of each camp also diverges. Usually the critics are economic liberals and the defenders are economic conservatives, although after his defeat in 1964 Barry Goldwater did urge a realignment of parties to provide the conservative viewpoint with more clear-cut representation and election choice. Even the major methodological flaw in each side's argument contributes to increasing the distance between the positions: many critics fatuously assume that the very goodness of their larger goals will somehow supply the elusive means by which their party reforms may be achieved, and many defenders smugly reflect the standpat conservatism of "whatever is, is right," and unthinkingly dismiss suggested changes as inherently futile.

In coming to one's own conclusions on the adequacy of the American party system, it clearly helps to tie the arguments on specific reforms back to their underlying normative premises. Awareness of the context and genealogy of a proposed change obviously enhances our understanding. Yet at the same time we run the risk of neglecting a close examination of the proposal by over-reacting to its premises. When the normative commitments of one side are irreconcilable to those of the other, that risk is aggravated. The normative dimension of the dispute over party must be handled carefully, therefore, lest it become a poor substitute for an analysis of the dispute itself.

Appropriate Reform Directions

Whatever one's appraisal of the party government doctrine, few deny that the critics have focused on a very real problem. It is stated by Pendleton Herring, whose study is perhaps the best single defense of the American government and party systems:

> With government now taking a larger role in all fields, the inadequacy of traditional institutions becomes apparent. Our governmental institutions do not provide any agency primarily designed to formulate and enact a national program. . . . If the political party is concerned chiefly with gaining office and if pressure groups devote their time to pursuing their special interests, how can we provide for the formulation of public policy so as to advance the welfare of all? Can we expect policy designed in the public interest to emerge from this diversity?[11]

Practicable reforms to remedy this problem must meet the following

---

[11] Herring, *The Politics of Democracy*, p. 107.

standards. They would be unrealistic paper exercises if they advocated drastic changes in the party system while retaining the present institutional context, or if they proposed extensively to alter formal institutional and constitutional arrangements. Realizable reforms, therefore, must link to and capitalize on whatever centralizing tendencies currently exist. The CPP's prognosis on the impact of nationalizing political forces meets this criterion; it promises gradual party changes in response to environmental changes. Let us speculate a bit on the logical implications of the CPP's position on the point.

Since a party's policies reflect in part its interest composition, voters would have greater policy choice if each major party attracted different sets of interests. In Michigan, for example, the Democrats strongly tend to be the metropolitan-urban party and the Republicans the suburban-rural party. Were this alignment projected nationally, each party's electoral following would be composed of distinctive interests whose geographical distribution would determine the proportions of two-party and one-party districts. Note that such a realignment does not overlook the existing diversity of interests but simply relates it to the parties differently than at present.

Continuing our speculation, we may assume that a legislator will be most responsive to factors that determine his re-election chances. Under what conditions, then, will he adhere most frequently to his party's position? Surely a legislator must oppose his party if its policy provokes intense majority hostility in his district. Such hostility typically indexes a sectional outlook. Two conditions of its diminution, therefore, are a dilution of the forces sustaining sectionalism or a rise to prominence of national issues provoking national rather than sectional reactions, or both. Wedding a legislator more firmly to his party's position requires, in addition, that his election fate depend less on the parochial interests of his district and more on his standing with the national party or the president. The district electorate in judging the legislator must be willing to focus on the important national issues instead of on purely local matters.

Restated more systematically, these speculations encompass the following conditions:

1. The mix of interests in most states and districts becomes more similar, and approaches a uniform diversity.
2. Most voters perceive the same national issues as the salient political issues, and these issues are not of a kind to promote sectional responses.

3. Each major party attracts a set of consistent interests different from the other party's set.
4. Interparty competition in presidential, congressional, and state politics becomes close in most states and districts.
5. To heighten the influence of the national party on a legislator's election chances, the authority of the national party organization is strengthened and voters' decisions reflect a judgment of the legislator's behavior on the salient national issues and on his record of party loyalty.

These conditions stipulate developments we may anticipate if the CPP's thesis on the existence and influence of nationalizing political forces proves to be correct. The present indeterminateness of that thesis, because of the newness and uneven penetration of these forces, is underscored by our discussion earlier in this chapter. Thus we must close on a note of uncertainty, which is perhaps not out of character in social science attempts to predict major change. Reader and author alike can take some consolation, however, from the fact that the confirming or disconfirming evidence on the nationalizing-forces argument should be forthcoming well within our lifetimes.

Further Reading

These suggestions for additional reading make no pretense at being exhaustive, either in party topics covered or in titles within each topic. To keep the listing within the bounds of some reason, I have arbitrarily chosen to cite only book publications, not articles. The focus of each work cited should be evident through a reading of the title or of the running commentary.

Among the better attempts to develop comparative party analysis across national boundaries are Maurice Duverger, *Political Parties* (New York: John Wiley & Sons, 1954) and Avery Leiserson, *Parties and Politics* (New York: Alfred A. Knopf, 1958). Although the following is less comparative than might be hoped for, it is of considerable use: Sigmund Neumann (ed.), *Modern Political Parties* (Chicago: University of Chicago Press, 1956). For a stimulating application of economic-style analysis of the mutual dependency of parties and voters, based on an instrumental concept of political rationality, see Anthony Downs, *An Economic Theory of Democracy* (New York: Harper & Brothers, 1957).

The ablest historical account of American parties, within reasonable length, is that of Wilfred Binkley, *American Political Parties* (New York: Alfred A. Knopf, 4th edit., 1962). A helpful account of the early period is William N. Chambers, *Political Parties in a New Nation* (New York: Oxford University Press, 1963). The most advanced textbook on American parties, which incorporates much original analysis, is V. O. Key, Jr., *Politics, Parties and Pressure Groups* (New York: Thomas Y. Crowell Company, 5th edit., 1964). Another textbook, unusual for the clarity with which it sets forth the normative criteria it applies, is Austin Ranney and Willmoore

Kendall, *Democracy and the American Party System* (New York: Harcourt, Brace and Company, 1956).

V. O. Key reinvigorated the field of state politics, long dormant under the weight of a highly traditional institutional-legal approach. His two major studies in this respect are *Southern Politics* (New York: Alfred A. Knopf, 1949) and *American State Politics: An Introduction* (New York: Alfred A. Knopf, 1956). Among subsequent studies by others which are effective analyses of their respective substantive topics *and* seek to contribute to an analysis of parties are: Alexander Heard, *A Two-Party South?* (Chapel Hill, University of North Carolina Press, 1952); Allan P. Sindler, *Huey Long's Louisiana: State Politics, 1920-1952* (Baltimore: Johns Hopkins Press, 1956); Leon D. Epstein, *Politics in Wisconsin* (Madison: University of Wisconsin Press, 1958); Duane Lockard, *New England State Politics* (Princeton: Princeton University Press, 1959).

Helpful accounts of other aspects of state politics include: Coleman B. Ransone, Jr., *The Office of Governor in the United States* (University, Alabama: University of Alabama Press, 1956); Malcolm E. Jewell (ed.), *The Politics of Reapportionment* (New York: Atherton Press, 1962); Malcolm E. Jewell, *The State Legislature* (New York: Random House, 1962); and John C. Wahlke *et al.*, *The Legislative System* (New York: John Wiley & Sons, 1962).

The following are but a few of the many titles which could be suggested on the general themes of party organization and campaign tactics: Huge Bone, *Party Committees and National Politics* (Seattle: University of Washington Press, 1958); Paul T. David *et al.*, *The Politics of National Party Conventions* (Washington: Brookings Institution, 1960); Gerald Pomper, *Nominating the President* (Evanston: Northwestern University Press, 1963); Nelson W. Polsby and Aaron B. Wildavsky, *Presidential Elections: Strategies of American Electoral Politics* (New York: Charles Scribner's Sons, 1964); and, on financing and contributions, Alexander Heard, *The Costs of Democracy* (Chapel Hill, University of North Carolina Press, 1960).

Two good examples of quantitative analysis of congressional roll-call alignments are: Julius Turner, *Party and Constituency* (Baltimore: Johns Hopkins Press, 1952) and Duncan McCrae, Jr., *Dimensions of Congressional Voting* (Berkeley: University of California Press, 1958). David B. Truman carefully analyzes many aspects of legislative behavior, and the influence of party and president thereon, in *The Congressional Party* (New York: John Wiley & Sons, 1959). A variety of approaches and methodologies is used in Donald R. Matthews, *U.S. Senators and Their World* (Chapel Hill: University of North Carolina Press, 1960), while veteran journalist William S. White conveys the "club" tone of Senate operations in *Citadel* (New York: Harper & Brothers, 1956). A full, but mostly descriptive, account of procedures and practices is offered by Bertram M. Gross,

The Legislative Struggle (New York: McGraw-Hill Book Company, 1953); somewhat more conceptual and systematic is William J. Keefe and Morris S. Ogul, *The American Legislative Process* (Englewood Cliffs, N.J.: Prentice-Hall, 1964).

Three important studies, each different in approach, treat mass electoral behavior. Bernard Berelson *et al.*, *Voting* (Chicago, University of Chicago Press, 1954), applies the sociological and demographic approach, based on sample survey analysis. In the last chapter the authors, who are empirical social scientists, try to relate their findings to normative political theory. In *The Future of American Politics* (New York: Harper & Brothers, 1951), Samuel Lubell combines personal interviewing, close study of election statistics, and shrewd judgment to assess vote trends in group-related terms. Angus Campbell *et al.*, *The American Voter* (New York: John Wiley & Sons, 1960) provides the fullest conceptual and interpretative account to date of the Survey Research Center's continuing analysis of mass electoral behavior, which heavily stresses psychological factors, especially that of party identification.

A good account of the lineage of the party reform position, as well as of its variations and inner logic, may be found in Austin Ranney, *The Doctrine of Responsible Party Government* (Urbana: University of Illinois Press, 1956). In addition to the CPP *Report*, to which frequent reference was made in the present volume, the following titles set forth more of the critics' position. In *Congress on Trial* (New York: Harper & Brothers, 1949), James M. Burns really indicts the party system, while in *The Deadlock of Democracy* (Englewood Cliffs, N.J.: Prentice-Hall, 1963) he develops the thesis that the gap between presidential and legislative wings in effect creates a four-party system. E. E. Schattschneider, perhaps the most influential spokesman in this country on behalf of the party reform doctrine, should be read closely in his brief, but tightly written *Party Government* (New York: Rinehart & Company, 1942). Two of the ablest defenses of the current party system are: Pendleton Herring, *The Politics of Democracy* (New York: Rinehart & Company, 1940) and Arthur N. Holcombe, *Our More Perfect Union* (Cambridge: Harvard University Press, 1950).

Index